"CHILDREN
From
HEAVEN"

TCHOUKI G. L. MINER

authorHOUSE®

AuthorHouse™
1663 Liberty Drive
Bloomington, IN 47403
www.authorhouse.com
Phone: 1 (800) 839-8640

Published by AuthorHouse 02/29/2020

ISBN: 978-1-7283-2311-4 (sc)
ISBN: 978-1-7283-2310-7 (e)

For the nature of evil is how subtly and cruelly it deceives us.
It is a terrible fact of life, and the sad state of the human condition that otherwise
really good people can still be responsible for the most terrible things.

PROLOGUE

Carl Jung wrote in his book "The Phenomenology of the Self" that "as men of science we have to acknowledge the reality of evil".

I became deeply interested in the Middle East after a brief visit to Haifa and Nazareth while traveling on a ship that stopped in the Haifa port. Subsequently I traveled on numerous occasions to Israel, the West Bank and Gaza Strip in the 1990's. After viewing many TV news reports and reading books and articles on the Middle East conflict, and its history, I was compelled to give an account of the many conversations I had, on these visits to the Holy Land, with both Palestinian and Israeli people.

The following pages are an attempt to give an outline of the unusual historical background, and present information which attests to the amazing intractability of the Arab-Israeli conflict.

Golda Meir wrote in her biography how she and her fellow Zionists, just prior to 1948, and while in the U.S. presenting their case for a Jewish state, secretly purchased all the metal parts of a dairy farm that had gone out of business. These they transported to Israel and were able to create arms from these metal parts that had been used to produce milk. And that is how the war of 1948 was executed by Israel. The early Zionists were prohibited from introducing arms in any way into Palestine. The Zionists formed their own army secretly while still under the British Mandate, the Palmach, which became the Haganah. In 1948, this military body swooped down on the whole area of what is now Israel proper (they must have appeared as a flock of evil birds to the Arabs) and, at gunpoint, forcibly removed all non-Jews to the West Bank and border of Gaza where they were instructed in arabic "uhrub" or "flee", in english, in the war fought in 1948. This last information is corroborated in the book, "How Israel Lost Its Soul" by Maxim Khalil, a French Jew of Lebanese origin who serviced in the Knesset in the 1950's.

Reportedly, at the same time, the Grand Mufti of Jerusalem told all Arabs to leave Palestine ostensibly because the armies of the Arab world would come to their aid and drive the Zionists "into the sea". Many Arabs did leave under these conditions, believing that they would be returning to their homes after this aim was achieved. The Grand Mufti, it should be noted, was a particularly odious person who actually traveled to Germany to visit and speak with Hitler who he appeared to admire. Hitler gave him a brief audience in which he refused to shake the Muftis's hand because he was an Arab.

While one can appreciate the good will and efforts for peace of the Jews who, on the eve of the Israeli signing of the document announcing their statehood, went out in cars with loudspeakers and attempted to dissuade Palestinian Arabs from leaving Palestine, saying, "wait, and see, we can work this out". But to what end was this attempt, when such Jewish people seemed oblivious to the fact that at that very moment, Arabs were being forced out of their homes at gunpoint by the Haganah?

I can never forget the article I read in New Yorker magazine many years ago, in the 1980's. The writer had visited Israel and, in a kibbutz, as he began a discussion on the current crisis, one of the men being interviewed, said, with great emotion, "we never wanted this suffering, this conflict, this bloodshed. These terrible things were never, never what we anticipated or imagined happening." And the man wept bitterly. How sadly, the Jewish state has held on, in spite of the unending suffering for both communities, caused by the political separatism, i.e. separate states for Arabs and Jews, most Israelis still cling to, to this day. This "political separatism" referred to is based on the fact that a group of Jews from the West came to Palestine in 1948, and before, with the intention of creating a separatist Jewish, and finally what became, a Jewish supremacist state superimposed on Palestine. The Jews from the West called themselves "zionists" which is a religious term although many were not specifically religious. Golda Meir, for example was an agnostic and David Ben Gurion, held to be the founder of the Jewish state was not a particularly religious man. Philosopher Yeshayahu Leibowitz considered Ben-Gurion "to have hated Judaism more than any other *man* he had met". The last quote is from Ben Gurion Wikipedia.

Subsequent, to the military action of the Zionists, homes in Palestine were confiscated by the Zionists. While walking through an area of shops and cafes in west Jerusalem, a Palestinian friend pointed out to me all the houses that now made up these Jewish shops and cafes which were formerly the homes of Arab families and had been confiscated or stolen, by the zionists in this "War of Independence" waged against the unarmed population of Palestine.

Consider the following excerpt in a now famous letter of Ben Gurion to his son, Amos.

"Negev land is reserved for Jewish citizens, whenever and wherever they want... we must expel Arabs and take their places... and if we have to use force, then we have the force at our disposal...". David Ben Gurion in 1937 letter to his son.

But later Benny Morris, an Israeli historian, pointed out Ben Gurion also said in the letter, **"there is enough room for us and for the Arabs in the land** [of Israel]. **And if we will have to use force, not for the sake of evicting the Arabs of the Negev or Transjordan, but rather in order to secure the right that belongs to us to settle there, force will be available to us."**

Quotes are from UK Media Watch.

The former quote of Ben Gurion is often pointed out as the intent of Israel to ethnically cleanse Palestine. However the second part of the letter, often not quoted, does bring a softening of Ben Gurion's approach and tone to the Palestinian population and the recognized need of Israel to coexist with the Arabs of Palestine. Yet this later statement is not very different in the actual stated intention of Israel, which is, one way or another, to ensure Israeli control over Palestine, and the manner that would be utilized was by force or militarily, as necessary. Absent from Gurion's statement is a clear moral basis for the imperative of a Jewish state, ending simply with a proclamation of Israel's inherent right to possess Palestine.

The following document that Ben Gurion reportedly hid in a secret file has recently been discovered and made public, show horrific genocidal acts on the part of the Israelis in the village of Sa is'.

"On February 15, 1948, a Palmach unit entered the village during the night and, without resistance, planted explosives against some of the houses. It was reported at the time that ten or more houses were totally or partially destroyed and 11 villagers were killed (5 of them small children). According to the official history of the Haganah, the village had been used as a base for Arab fighters. However, press reports at the time ... belie this, since the Palmach units met "without opposition" in the village. According to Benvenisti (who gives the date of the attack as 14 February), the Palmach units that raided Sa is' killed 60 people and demolished 16 houses."

Above paragraph quoted from Wikipedia.

The Palmach referred to above, was the Jewish resistance that formed itself under the British Mandate and was really the first army of Israel. The Haganah was considered the legitimate army of Israel under Ben Gurion and the new Israeli government. The Irgun, though not mentioned in the description of the massacre at Sa is', was outlawed by Ben Gurion's government yet its genocidal practices continued in many instances, such as the massacre at Deir Yassin.

In a youtube interview with Ilan Pappe, noted Israeli historian and scholar, who has written extensively on Israeli ethnic cleansing of Palestinians, recounts the massacres at Sa'sa'. He describes how Israeli forces in 1948 entered the village, rounded up 60 men, took them to a ravine and then "dangled" them over it before killing them. The Israelis then set fire to the village even though they knew there were people sleeping in the houses.

"We came to this country which was already populated by Arabs, and we are establishing a Hebrew, that is a Jewish state here. In considerable areas of the country we bought lands from the Arabs. Jewish villages were built in the place of Arab villages. You do not even know the names of these Arab villages, and I do not blame you, because these geography books no longer exist; not only do the books not exist, the Arab villages are not there either. Nahalal arose in the place of Mahalul, Gevat — in the place of Jibta, Sarid — in the place of Haneifs and Kefar Yehoshua — in the place of Tell Shaman. There is no one place built in this country that did not have a former Arab population."

Above quoted from a speech made by Moshe Dayan in Wikipedia.

Consider the following: "Almost daily from 1937, at the same time that Nazi thugs were terrorizing European Jews, the Zionist gangs of Jewish foreigners executed 'calculated campaigns of terror' on the indigenous Palestinians.

Palestinians were mercilessly slaughtered, maimed and terrorized by repeated bombings or attacks with machine guns and grenades on Palestinian cafés, on 'casual pedestrians', on

Palestinian vehicles and buses, passenger trains, orphanages, schools, shops, Arab markets and quarters. Jewish gangs raided Arab villages, planted landmines, in Nazi-style coldbloodedly executed rounded up villagers, and the Irgun Zvai Leumi, à la Saudi extremism, ramped up the terror by threatening 'to cut off Arab hands raised against the Jewish cause'" From the Palestine Chronicle, August 2019.

I have heard from people in Israel, from both international workers and read from the files of human rights reports as well as from conversations with Palestinians about unspeakable atrocities committed by Israel against the Palestinians. It is also true that some Palestinians have committed brutal acts of violence and terrorism against Israelis. In one case, Palestinians terrorists hijacked a Swedish airline in the 1960's and murdered the captain. Obviously these cruel and mindless acts of terrorism do nothing to legitimize the certainly reasonable cause of Palestinian statehood and security. One notorious and particularly vicious Palestinian terrorist, Abu Nidal spent more of his time murdering Palestinians who he accused of collaborating with Israel than those acts of terrorism he plotted and carried out against Israelis.

The world was horrified by the murders of the Israelis at the hands of Palestinian terrorists at Munich's 1972 Olympic Games. Oddly, German secret services had been warned by a Palestinian contact in Lebanon that the attack on Israelis performing at the Olympics could take place. Unaccountably, the intel was ignored and for forty years Germany has guarded the facts surrounding their responsibility for the atrocity that took place. When Israelis speak of their "right to the Holy Land", and are reminded of the destruction of homes and properties of Palestinians; (for Israel to become a nation) and that "two wrongs don't make a right", (Jewish claims of the holocaust to justify their militarism) so the same can be said of the Palestinians who, with impunity destroyed Israeli lives and so at the very same time, destroyed all credibility for Palestinian justice, in the eyes of many. Abu Daoud, alleged to have planned the massacres claimed that Yasser Arafat, though he did not plan the attacks, endorsed them. Daoud claimed that Arafat saw the five Palestinian terrorists off with his blessing, saying, "God protect you". One of the most ignominious Palestinian terrorists, one Abu Nidal, was also accused of plotting the Munich massacres.

CHAPTER 1

One of the most truly horrifying atrocities to come out of the crisis and conflict in the region, was the murder of Vittorio Arrigoni who was an Italian peace activist and blogger working with the International Solidarity Movements in Gaza. He provided immeasurable support to the Gazans and also to the Palestinians in Lebanese refugee camps. He was well-known for comforting children who had lost their parents or other loved ones from intermittent, though constant, Israeli bombardments. He played sports, such as volleyball with young people and was totally engaged in their activities with them. He was committed to ending the racial discriminatory practices of Israel and supported a state where all people of the region possessed equal political rights.

For all these actions, Vittorio was much loved by Gazans. In April, 2011 he was abducted by an ultra extremist group, "The Brigade of the Gallant Companion of the Prophet Mohammed bin Muslima," a Palestinian Salafist group, Al-Snajib. He (Arrigoni) was shown on a video on YOUTube, blindfolded with blood around his eyes. His captors said that he would be killed if their leader, held by the Gazan government, Walid al Maqdisi, was not released in 30 hours. For reasons that are unclear, his body was found, hang in a house in northern Gaza, even before the deadline had expired, by Gazan security men. All Palestinian factions condemned the killing. An official statement from Hamas described the murder of Vittorio as a horrible act committed by an "an outlawed and mentally deviated group". Similar shocked reports came from Fatah, Islamic Jihad and the Palestinian Authority as well as the government of Italy and the United Nations.

It can be said that the crisis in Palestine has created the most morally revolting, virulent, and fanatic Muslim (so-called) extremists in the history of the Islamic world. Al-Qaeda did not exist until a few decades ago and is rumored to actually have been created by the CIA during the former Afghanistan invasion by the Soviet Union in which the U.S. supported the Mujahideen in its own effort to gain a foothold in that region. Thirty or forty years ago, the extremist group responsible for Vittorio's death, did not exist, nor did other similar political groups, exist. "The Brigade" also claimed that since Vittorio came from an "infidel state," he had been "spreading corruption" in Gaza. Upon first hearing of this horrifying tragedy I knew immediately that the fanatics who murdered this wonderful person, Vittorio, had hated any non-Muslim who was committed to supporting justice for the Palestinians. The murderers want a world of "black and white" and hate the idea that there can be non-Muslims coming from the west who want justice in that region, as desperately and as fervently as Palestinians and other Arab people do. "The Brigade" and their murder of such an extraordinary peace activist is a staggering mockery of real Islam. The murder of Vittorio Arrigoni was a heinous and mindless crime, unprecedented in the history of Islam.

These Arab and Muslim fanatical groups did not exist as has been pointed out, in recent decades past. Many analysts say that these groups came into existence in direct counterpoint to the hawkish policies of the Israeli government. There can be no doubt that the group who murdered Vittorio, as well as Islamic Jihad, Al Aqsa Mosque Brigade and Salafism would not have ever have existed if it were not for the Zionist movement and its occupation in Palestine.

There were also accusations of Israeli involvement in the murder of Vittorio Arrigoni as well as in the murder of an Israeli activist in Jenin by unknown masked gunmen. Both Hamas spokesmen and a German politician Inge Hoger, said that Israel could have profited from the two deaths in terms of deterring other activists from joining the peace flotilla about to sail to Gaza with the intention of breaking the Israeli blockade against Gaza.

CHAPTER 2

In Noam Chomsky's seminal work on the subject of the Middle East, "The United States, Israel and the Palestinians," he writes of an Israeli journalist, B. Rosenthal, who unearthed in German records concerning the Third Reich a letter from the Irgun, the outlawed army under Ben Gurion, entreating Hitler to join forces with the Irgun and Stern Gang, also a notorious and outlawed Israeli terrorist group, and work together with Hitler who would then create a totalitarian state in Europe, while the Irgun/Stern Gang would work to create a totalitarian and expanded between Palestinian borders, Jewish state in the Middle East. This letter was published twice, once in January and again in February in 1983 in "Haaretz", a newspaper which is published daily in Tel Aviv, in both Hebrew and in English. Further information on the origin of this letter, reveals that it was written by Avraham Stern, the founder of the Lehi, in Hebrew, and in english called the Stern Gang, which was considered terrorist and outlawed by David Ben Gurion. There were many accounts of the terrorism practiced by the Irgun and Stern gang. One horrific report was of members of the group on a rampage through the West Bank. An old man was sitting down outside his humble home to have lunch. As he began to eat his soup, a member of the Irgun strode by and shot him in the heart. The elderly man dropped dead instantly, his head falling into his lunch. This story is recounted in "O Jerusalem" by Larry Collins and Dominique Lapierre. These acts were designed to terrorize the Arab community and many Arab families did in fact, flee their homes, because of the nightmares they were suddenly subjected to by the Jewish terrorists.

The fanaticism of Stern caused him to break away from the Irgun, an actual army, whose continued terrorist activities were also banned by Ben Gurion. The letter was found after WWII ended by a British official in the German Embassy of Istanbul, Turkey. The latter data can be viewed in an online interview with Lenni Brenner and Stan Heller of TSVN, a U.S. cable TV network. Brenner is the author of "51 Documents", which details Zionist complicity with Nazism.

On the same subject and theme, Mahmoud Abbas published a book he wrote in 1984 entitled, "The Connection between Nazism and Zionism. He was accused of writing a book of "holocaust denial" by some. Although later he confirmed that the holocaust the Jews suffered under the Third Reich was a horrific atrocity and denied these accusations, he recently reiterated his claims that, similar to the letter published in Haaretz, there had been a kind of collaboration among some Zionists to use the holocaust to their advantage, which objective was to achieve a Jewish state.

Mr. Abbas is currently building himself a $13 million "palace" in Ramallah. According to Arab journalist Khaled Abu Toameh, the billions of dollars in aid benefit from the U.S. and other countries has done nothing to boost the peace process or improve the lives of Palestinians. The money appears to have gone straight into the pockets of Palestinian officials and in particular, Abbas himself. Toameh's comments were printed in an article published in the "Gatestone Institute". While it is true that conservative Israeli governments are responsible for stone-walling genuine peace between the two groups, that is hardly an excuse for the blatant corruption described in the previously referred to article and similar condemnations in the media of the PNA.

It enters the mind, upon reviewing this amazing letter discovered in the German Embassy in Istanbul after the war ended, and published in Haaretz, that Hitler's revenge can be seen in the atrocities of the Middle East by Israel, now a regional power, against the indigenous population of Palestine as a horrific and sickening continuation of the Third Reich itself.

I remember reading in a book on Middle East recent history how, the day the Israeli state was born with Golda Meir weeping with joy standing alongside David Ben Gurion, the orthodox rabbis in the Old City of Jerusalem shut themselves up in their ancient synagogues and went into mourning.

The region is filled with forces, historical, psychological and political that are so potent. The observer of Israeli domination of the region can not help but see how imminent is the threat of war, a war that could even lead, ultimately, to a war that would engulf the whole world.

CHAPTER 3

I met so many wonderful and interesting people when traveling in Israel, and also in the West Bank. I met many people I would like to have known better and become friends with.

It was a mystery to me how so many Israelis, good people and many I admired, could be willing to accept the theft (as it was proven to be) of a densely-populated Palestine. It was as though they were under some terrible spell. And the people who, as will be accounted further on, committed crimes against unarmed Palestinians, appear to be suffering from some virulent psychic infection.

Geo-political conflict or strategies, is a term often applied to Palestine by the media. But what are these geopolitical "strategies" referred to so frequently in discussions on the Middle East? And why is the persecution, and, according to some analysts, slow genocide of the Palestinian people so crucial to these said strategies?

To many, the answer is obvious. Israel wants the entire region of Palestine for its own state. The very continued existence of Palestinian people in their state or under Israeli occupation is a glaring reminder that Israel is a state based on theft.

The issue of a huge culture gap between the peoples of Palestine and Israel is very real. It is not understood in the west that there is more connection between Israelis of middleastern background, such as Iranian or Iraqi or Morrocan Jews, living in Israeli, and the Palestinians. One Iranian Israeli told me how his Palestinian employees thanked him profusely for his good manners and conduct toward them. In the Arab world there is a certain civility practiced in daily conduct among the people. In contrast the Jews from Europe and the west, living in Israel, are viewed as crass, insensitive and thoroughly unmannerly.

Gamal Nasser, leader of Egypt in the 1950's is quoted as saying that the problem in the modern state of Israel is that "they (the Jews) left brown and came back white". The Jews of the west, now present in Israel, are a completely different culture than any culture of the middleast or Arab world.

Most Americans have no idea how frequent and how high the rate of suicide is among Israeli soldiers. It can also be noted that the "brigs" or military prisons were filled with soldiers during the Second Intifada (which took place from September 2000 February 2005) who would rather stay in prison for months rather than commit the atrocities and illegalities Israeli soldiers were forced to perform under military orders at that time.

Referring to actual suicides, there were three after the last Gaza invasion, known in Israel as "Operation Protective Edge", in 2014. All three soldiers were found dead with their weapons beside them. Fifteen soldiers committed suicde in 2015. According to a report from the IDF, suicides among soldiers doubled in 2014. Three of these suicides were reported to be Ethiopean Jews. According to reports suicide is the reason most cited for Israeli soldiers' deaths, not combat or any other reason such as accidental deaths occuring while off duty.

The IDF has recently revealed closely guarded statistics. According to these reports from the military in Israel, twenty-four soldiers take their lives every year. The same reports state that 237 soldiers have taken their own lives in Israel in the past ten years.

CHAPTER 4

Secrets of the state of Israel are unusual and there is more than one.

But none more strange, by far, than is the story of Otto Skorzeny.

Skorzeny was a high ranking Nazi and favorite of Hilter. Skorzeny, like Hitler was not German but Austrian-born. It was Skorzeny that carried out the plot to rescue Mussolini when he was captured by the Italian government, who had become convinced Italy should align itself with the Allied Forces. Considered one of Skorzeny's greatest military achievements, the rescue took place in 1943. Skorzeny used a storch airplane to accomplish his risky rescue. Mussolini was taken to Rome and then Berlin. After WWII ended, the Mossad, Israel's intelligence agency contacted Skorzeny where he lived in Spain and worked to find safe places for former Nazi officials who would then reveal the whereabouts of hidden former Nazis. Skorzeny agreed to work for Mossad in exchange for being taken off the hit-list of targeted Nazis. Mossad also offered Skorzeny a good deal of money to work for them which Skorzeny declined, saying, that he had had enough money.

It was curious though apparent, that Skorzeny simply admired the skills of Mossad as a "killing machine". He quickly capitulated to giving his best military efforts to achieving whatever goals and aims Mossad set out before him. Otto Skorzeny appeared to find the ruthlessness of Mossad highly appealing. He eagerly joined Mossad when that organization promised to remove him from Israel's hit-list, even though American and British intelligence stated in their secret memos that Skorzeny was "the most dangerous man in europe". When Elie Weisel refused to remove Skorzeny from the hit-list, Mossad finally forged a document from him stating that Weisel had agreed to allow Skorzeny to live even though this document was a lie.

Upon Skorzeny's recruitment, he was taken by Mossad officials to visit Yad Vashem. Although respectful, Skorzeny showed no sign of shock or remorse whatsoever. During the visit a holocaust survivor recognized Skorzeny and called out that this man had caused the deaths of many Jews, specifically Hungarian Jews. Whereupon, the Mossad officials accompanying Skorzeny, assured the outraged man that he was mistaken and that Skorzeny was, in fact, a holocaust survivor himself.

Skorzeny, as his first assignment for Mossad in 1962, was hired as a bodyguard to Heinz Krug, a German scientist working for Egypt to help them create a bomb that would destroy Israel. Krug recognized Skorzeny as the well-known former Nazi official, and immediately hired him when he presented himself to Krug for his employ. But Skorzeny deceived Krug into meeting him in a deserted area outside Munich, where he shot and murdered Krug.

Born June 12, 1908 which is under the astrological sign of Gemini, or the "twins" and noted for its characteristic dualism, Skorzeny certainly lived up to the traits of his sign. He worked both for The Third Reich and Israel's Mossad with equal zeal.

Although Skorzeny stood before Dachau Military Tribunal he was acquitted. His charge was wearing a uniform of the enemy, a charge which is punishable by death. However, Skorzeny was released on a technicality. The charge of wearing a uniform while actually engaging in combat could not be proven. Also British Special Operations Yeo Thomas could not testify against Skorzeny as he had used the same illegal tactic, deceiving the enemy and wearing a fake enemy uniform behind enemy lines. Mysteriously, he escaped from the military camp where he was detained by the Germans with help, Skorzeny alleged, from the U.S.

Although he joined the Nazi party in his native Austria as a young man, he actually was involved in a military action which saved the life of the president of Austria from being killed by the Nazis in 1938, further illustrating his conflictive loyalties.

Dead of cancer in 1975, Otto s Mossad handler and trainer, Joe Raanan, flew at his own expense to the funeral of Otto Skorzeny in Spain. There were two funerals, one in Madrid, Spain where he had lived after the war and the other in Vienna where his family members were buried. Both funerals were complete with a very large group of former Nazi compatriots and their wives who stood at attention and made a full Nazi salute at the conclusion of the funeral ceremonies.

Thus ended the absolutely one hundred percent truly bizarre account of the life of Otto Skorzeny.

All of the information concerning the life of Otto Skorzeny is from Wikipedia online encyclopedia and from Tel Aviv s Hareetz newspaper, in an article published March 27, 2016.

CHAPTER 5

I watched a video created by a young woman of American Jewish background, Anna Baltzer, who is a member of an organization of women working to expose human rights violations and support Palestinians living under the Israeli occupation. She has also taught children in the West Bank. In this video, Anna articulately speaks of the conditions which most Palestinians in the West Bank live under.

First, she shows the roads, two roads in a video shot, one Israeli and the other Palestinian. The former is a modern, paved four-lane highway. The latter is an old road filled with rubble and unusable. Anna then discusses the checkpoints Palestinians have to pass through in order to travel to their jobs, often located inside Israel. Due to the Israeli occupation there is very little infrastructure and/or jobs in the West Bank. For a thirty mile drive, Palestinians are forced to wait in long lines at several checkpoints and what would normally take forty minutes by car can take up to eight hours due to forced delays for the IDF. Also, Anna points out that inside the West Bank there are many checkpoints which Palestinians must pass through, not to leave for Israel, but only to travel to other Palestinian villages. There is no security reason for the checkpoints inside the West Bank that any outside observer can ascertain.

The sole reason appears to be as an added harassment to the daily lives of Paletinians.

Israeli "settlements" or colonies in the West Bank are completely illegal under international law. Yet the Israeli government offers 100,000 shekels or over $20,000 to any Israeli who will go live in these illegal settlements. Often Palestinian farmers will wake up to see on a plateau over theirs flocks or fields of crops, several trailers of Israelis that have appeared overnight. These trailers over time become towns, other illegal settlements of Israeli citizens. Some of these Israelis are particularly vicious. There are reports of putting out the eye of a Palestinian child, of beating an old Palestinian woman with a cane, and of murdering a Palestinian. An Israeli man named David working with the international rights activists had his entire face beaten to a bloody pulp when he confronted the Israeli settlers over their cruel and criminal acts to Palestinians. Palestinians are forbidden under the Israeli laws they are now subject to, from being armed. Israelis are allowed by the same lawmakers of the Knesset, to arm themselves "to the hilt".

Another crucial issue addressed by Anna Baltzer in the same video, is the issue of a wall which often divides whole Palestinian villages while the Israeli settlements and their roads remain completely intact. Supporters of this wall urge and promote its validity, and point out that the rate of suicide bombers has noticeably dropped. But few Israelis acknowledge the fact that if the previously described severe restrictions on the Palestinians resulting in, for example, the tragic deaths of the precious, newborn twins denied immediate access to life sustaining incubators available only in Israeli hospitals, then there would be no Palestinians willing to sacrifice their lives in protest of the brutal conditions Palestinians are forced to live under.

Instead, Israeli settlers on their side of the wall, make embankments of upturned earth and fill them with flowers, thus disguising the harsh reality of the wall. And in this "disguising of the wall" Israelis hide as well, from the responsibility of turning aside any and all facts or information that would lead them to question, morally, the entire Israeli occupation, particularly in the West Bank where they reside, and, according to the UN, illegally.

CHAPTER 6

I recall while visiting the Jewish settlement in Hebron, entering a general store which sold food and other household supplies. I needed to buy a tube of toothpaste which I kept forgetting to do and assumed this shop would be as good as any other in which to make this purchase. To my surprise the man sitting at the counter reacted very hostilely to my request, abruptly stating that their store was not open to serving the needs of the general public, or words to that effect.

As I wandered through the settlement, I could not help but recall the feeling I had experienced many years ago, when I had lived for a short period of time in the then famous Haight-Ashbury neighborhood of San Francisco. Although the Haight district did not exhibit the violence of some of the members of the settlements as reported in many human rights journals, yet both the settlement and the Haight-Ashbury, the later in 1967, exuded a sense of wild excitement and exhilaration. Both people of both regions were convinced they had created a kind of "apocalyptic awakening". Unfortunately, in the case of the settlement in Hebron, the "awakening" was grievously marred by criminal violence and was certainly, in that regard, the opposite of the peace loving "flower children" who sought to delegitimize war as a means of conflict resolution and who wanted everything to be free, open and unrestrained.

Anna informs the viewers of her video that American taxpayers are footing the bill for these atrocities in Palestine. She clearly states the people of the West Bank do not want pity. They want protection, security of person and justice. They want to be able to live freely as they once did and their ancestors did, for centuries, in Palestine.

Anna, advises anyone who cares about justice to not buy any Israeli goods for sale in American markets and to write letters of protest to Congresspeople and Senators.

The critical point in this video of Anna Baltzer is that human rights violations in the West Bank aren't scattered or occasional. They are ongoing and very grave. Only Americans and Israelis exercising a concerted political will can change the nightmares just described that Palestinians experience on a daily basis.

Once again, the reader confronts the fact that the above information would never be presented on any mainstream, western TV stations.

CHAPTER 7

When I lived in a remote area of Mallorca, Spain, from 1992 until 1995, I subscribed to Time magazine and would read every single article every week. Being the european Time, it was not exactly the same articles as those published in Time magazine in the United States. To understand exactly the difference, see youtube video of Anna Baltzer showing Time, the same month replacing an article on Palestinian violations in the european copy with a completely different story, in the U.S. publication I remember reading about an attempt on the part of several highranking IDF members to actually take over the government of Israel. But their plot was foiled by Mossad and they were assassinated. The account reminded me of the men in the S.S., Hitler's army, who attempted to eliminate Hitler and were themselves caught and executed. There are so many things going on inside Israel that the international community is unaware of. Certainly people in the western countries are completely unaware of such a coup right inside Israel by Israeli soldiers themselves.

I also read in the same publication, an account of an Arab mayor in Bethlehem who refused to give his mayorship to the Israeli appointed to his job when Israel took over the West Bank in the late 1960 s. The mayor, still tenaciously clinging to his post, went out one morning and got into his car to drive to his office. The car blew up. Though the man survived the Israeli bombing of his car, he lost both legs.

This account clearly show, and it goes without saying, that most Americans would be shocked and horrified if they had real information of the extent of concerted, premeditated violence by Israeli authorities against the Palestinians, carried out without heart or conscience. How is it possible for Israel to be considered a democracy? Why is Israel frequently referred to as part of the family of nations, on the part of the west?

CHAPTER 8

In a book entitled "The General's Son", Miko Peled, the author, told of how his mother, could have had a lovely home in Jerusalem after the war in 1948. But when she heard that the Arab owners now lived in a refugee camp she refused. Listening to an online video in which Miko Peled spoke of visiting his now ninety year old mother who still lives in Jerusalem, he related how she used to tell of walking, as a teenage girl, in what is now West Jerusalem and see all the Arab families sitting and relaxing in front of their homes. She says how ashamed she felt when the 1948 War broke out and all these people were driven out of their homes and many forced to live in refugee camps. Peled's father, a decorated general turned peacemaker, declared after the 1967 war that Israel chose to make that war with the Arabs. That, in fact, there had been no "existential" threat to Israel. Peled's grandfather, Avraham Katsnelson was one of the signer's of Israel's Declaration of Independence. This information is a critical slice of information about the few Israelis, and in particular the prominent Israeli Peled family, willing to tell the truth about the past sixty years.

Mattiyahu, or "Matti" Peled, was the father of Miko Peled. As a youth in Jerusalem under British occupation, he was a member of the Palmach, a secret military group of Jews devoted to creating the Jewish state. Matti Peled then became a general in the 1948 War of Independence in which Israeli military forces, the Haganah, drove out or caused to flee about one million Palestinians.

In 1967, General Peled was part of the military attack and occupation of the West Bank and Gaza. Later, General Peled claimed that Israel was not threatened militarily at that time by the armies of other Arab countries, but rather took possession of the West Bank because of necessary economic and military strategies, that General Peled supported. Over time it became apparent that the real reason for invading the West Bank in 1967, was Israel's harsh and rigid obsession with security and the desire to make these areas "de facto" inclusions into the Israeli state. After the occupation of these areas, and fully opposing a continuing occupation of the West Bank, Peled proposed to the Israeli government that the West Bank, a contiguous area at that time, become a sovereign Palestinian state, with both Israel and the Palestinian state he proposed, sharing Jerusalem. But certain government agencies already had plans for Israeli "settlements" to dot the region. In 1975, along with other dissident Israeli journalists and knesset members, General Peled formed the Israeli Council for Peace between Israelis and Palestinians. It was at this time, that the Council presented a proposal for a Palestinian state with full sovereign rights, which was rejected outright by the Israeli government. The ICPIP proposal was considered very radical and the group sued a newspaper columnist who labelled the ICPIP anti-Zionist.

CHAPTER 9

Many people criticized Yasser Arafat for rejecting the peace proposal offered by Ehud Barak and brokered by then President Clinton in 2000 at Camp David, but the fact was, Arafat and the Palestinian people were never offered a real state. They were offered a "cheese-hole" slice of territory filled with Israeli settlements that would have still continued to be have been under Israeli control. In the face of the international community who wanted the Palestinians to accept this cheese-hole state, Arafat did show real courage. It is amazing to note that even in one of the worst conflicts imaginable, i.e. the Arab-Israeli conflict, the desire for communication is so strong in human beings, that albeit the dire circumstance, and out of the most extreme necessity, Israeli officials spoke with Yasser Arafat, even though to do so was illegal at the time they met and spoke. The two parties met secretly for many years before the Israeli government declared it was "legal" to openly speak with Arafat.

It is very sad to say that according to Wikipedia, and other sources both inside and outside the Palestinian community, Arafat had amassed a fortune in contributions that he clearly did not use to assist Palestinians in creating a quality infrastructure in the Palestinian communities. Gaza in particular, continued to be impoverished and the funds to create a much improved life for the residents were not utilized. Arafat took the VAT tax from goods purchased by Palestinians and deposited directly this money into his personal bank account, Bank Leumi, in Tel Aviv. Then, in an apparent counterclaim to Palestinian VAT tax deposited into Arafat's personal account, an IMF audit concluded that he and the PNA used the funds to invest in Palestinian assets. The audit concluded there were no improprieties involved in the investments where the monies were channeled.

However, in 2003, Arafat's own finance ministry hired American accountants whose findings claimed that Arafat had a secret portfolio in the amount of $1 billion. It was further reported that Arafat and the PLO had assets of $10 billion even while Arafat publicly claimed to be bankrupt. According to Dennis Ross, former Middle East negotiators under Presidents Bush and Clinton, Arafat lived a modest life but had vast financial connections referred to as "neopatrimonialism". Salam Fayyad, a former World Bank official whom Arafat himself appointed as Finance Minister of the PNA in 2002, claimed that Arafat s secret financial business dealings harmed Palestinians, particularly in Gaza, where the population was very poor. Condemning outright Arafat's business practices, Fayyad said that Arafat used from Palestinian monies $20 million to pay PNA security services in Gaza alone, instead of investing in badly needed infrastructure in Gaza.

Arafat's wife, Suha Tawil, a Christian Arab from a wealthy background, was over thirty years younger than Arafat. She publicly made statements saying she viewed her marriage to Arafat as a mistake and should never have married him. She tried to leave him on numerous occasions but was prevented by Arafat from doing so. These statements were made in an article published in London's Guardian newspaper in 2004. Mrs. Arafat went on to say she loved her husband but life with him was far more difficult than she had anticipated, and explained that due to stringent security measures they were forced under, she had "lost her identity".

Numerous Palestinians I spoke to told me that they did not support Yassir Arafat. I cannot claim to have spoke to all the Palestinians in Israel and the West Bank, but it did appear to me that roughly half of the Palestinians I spoke to did not support him while the other half did. When I wrote letters for the Urgent Action Network for Amnesty International I received information one week on the imprisonment of Iyad El Sarraj, a prominent and well-known Gazan psychiatrist. In this report Dr. Sarraj accounted how he had accused the Palestinian Authority and Yassir Arafat of corruption in an interview while visiting New York City. Upon return he had been taken to jail for a short time. When he was released Dr. Sarraj then wrote a kind of letter of apology to Arafat. Immediately he was seized again by the Palestinian police and incarcerated for a whole month during which time, he said, "he feared for his life". Finally Dr. Sarraj was released. I had always considered Yassir Arafat to be a reasonable political leader of the Palestinians, however after reading this information, I was never able to support him again.

To call Yasser Arafat an "autocrat" would be putting it both mildly and too nicely

CHAPTER 10

Marwan Barghouti is a man who was tried for multiple murders in 2001, and found guilty in Israeli court, although Barghouti claims he is innocent of the charges. He refused legal defense alleging that the entire proceedings of the court were illegal. Mr. Barghouti denies giving direct orders for the seven assassinations he is accused of. Among the Israelis and the Palestinians, there are continuous murder plot and counter murder plots on both sides. Because of his widespread support among Palestinians, Israel suspects that Barghouti could provide credible leadership for his people. Some observers believe this is the real reason Barghouti was indicted and is now in "deep freeze"; i.e. Barghouti is serving so many consecutive life sentences, that under his current sentencing and incarceration, he can never be released. There is currently no other political figure among Palestinians who enjoys more support as a leader, than Marwan Barghouti. Thus he is the greatest threat to Israeli domination and presents the greatest possibility for a viable Palestinian state, the last thing Israel wants.

In an online publication, the people's voice.org, on April 24, 2012, Stephen Lendman writes:

"Barghouti is a political prisoner. On May 20, 2004, he was wrongfully convicted of involvement in three terrorist attacks killing five people. Acquitted on 33 other charges, he received five consecutive life sentences plus 40 years.

A three-judge panel ruled that although he didn't fully control local Brigade leaders and wasn't directly involved, he had "significant influence" over their conduct.

In other words, no evidence existed. A legitimate court would have acquitted him. Israel's military one judged him guilty by accusation. Due process and judicial fairness were absent. Virtually all prosecuted Palestinians face the same fate, including children."

"... He (Barghouti) 'never denied the right of the Jewish people to a Jewish state.' He also 'expressed contempt for Islamic fundamentalists.' Above all, he's incorruptible, he added. Many Israelis support him for good reason. He wants Palestinian sovereignty respected, as well as even-handed diplomatic peace talks.

Theatrics and false publicity substituted for judicial fairness. Barghouti never had a chance. His legal rights were violated. Numerous international laws were breached. The entire process was illegitimate. Guilty as charged damned him to five consecutive life sentences plus 40 years.

Eight years later, he faces new charges after the fact. They're just as spurious as what got him convicted. Putting him away for life isn't enough. Beating up on him relentlessly continues."

In 1996, although elected to the Palestinian Legislative Council, Barghouti actively campaigned against the corruption of Yasser Arafat's administration and human rights violations by its security forces. He also established relationships with Israeli politicians and was said to have the phone numbers of half the Knesset. He also had strong involvements with members of Israeli peace organizations. His position was that of advocating continued armed resistance to Israeli occupation but condemned attacks on civilian targets inside Israel. Many prominent Palestinian figures have campaigned for his release as well as members of the European parliament. Many claim that among other reasons, Barghouti´s arrest was illegal because he was arrested in an area that was outside Israeli jurisdiction. According to polls sixty percent of Palestinians support Barghouti as their leader. If there were a vote today for a new president for the Palestinian Authority, Barghouti would win over both Mahmoud Abbas and Hamas leader, Ismail Haniyeh, according to polls.

Marwan Barghouti currently calls for a third intifada. But it is a Gandhiinspired nonviolent uprising that would thoroughly discredit Israel who consistently has claimed that all Palestinian operations (to liberate themselves from the oppression and tyranny of Israeli policies toward Palestinians) are terrorist. In 2001 Mossad kidnapped Barghouti and held him in detention for 100 days during which he was interrogated and tortured. Israeli authorities then held him in solitary confinement for 1,000 days in a tiny cell infested with rats and cockroaches. Barghouti´s continued denial of the charges against him and commitment to the original 1967 borders for the Palestinians state plus his unwavering commitment to achieving a Palestinians state have earned him the title, "the Nelson Mandela of Palestine" by many in the media, among Arabs and international rights activists.

It is clear from his non-violent and uncompromising stance in refusing to concede territorial boundaries, Barghouti is a man of integrity in the eyes of the international community. He was nominated for the Nobel Peace prize in this year by none other than South Africa's Bishop Desmond Tutu, himself a Nobel laureate in 1984 and consistent opponent of Israeli policy toward Palestinians.

CHAPTER 11

It is incredible to see that after over sixty years of conflict in Palestine, the leaders of the country are the most hawkish and least likely to achieve a serious peace in the region. Watching on CNN a debate program presented by the thoughtful and often salient Fareed Zakaria, one guest remarked that Avigdor Lieberman, the former deputy minister of Israel, now defense minister, has the view that all Arabs should be expelled from Israel and the West Bank. As such, his position is thoroughly racist, obviously, and thus has no credibility with the international community. Mr. Lieberman brazenly places himself completely at odds with the international community in terms of creating a Palestinian state and his position prohibits long term peace with the Arabs of Palestine.

Many people in the west are not aware of a Jewish religious group, "Neturei Karta" which refuses to acknowledge the Israeli state and publicly opposes it. They have a very beautiful synagogue and study hall in Jerusalem, and some members of Neturei Karta even live in Israel, in the neighborhood of Mea Shearim, a notably ultra conservative and orthodox area, as well as other areas in Israel. Formed seventy-eight years ago, they actively oppose Zionism and have also been known to make statements in support of known Islamic extremists. Their name means "Guardian of the City" in Aramaic and is derived from the Jerusalem Torah. They believe they teach true Torah principles. They believe that only the Messiah can restore the state of Israel. The sect also believes it is blasphemous to create a secular political state; that such an action is in complete opposition to the teaching of the Torah. They actively support Palestinian rights. The members of Neturei Karta can be seen in protests against Israel in the U.S., in Turkey, and in England, as well as other countries, holding signs and placards that advocate boycotting Israeli goods. Regarded as a "wild fringe" in other orthodox circles, the members of this group are mainly derived from Hungarian Jews who arrived in Palestine in the nineteenth century. They resented the non-religious Jews who, under the Ottoman Empire, began the Zionist struggle. They have even been known to burn the Israeli flag in public demonstrations against Israel. One of the leaders of N.K., served as a cabinet minister for Jewish Affairs in the PLO, Moshe Hirsch.

I also recall reading in Time magazine an article about a young Palestinian who attempted a suicide bombing but was unsuccessful. He was rushed to an Israeli hospital where his life was saved. The kindness and caring showed him by the Israeli medical staff (who realized that most likely his attempted bombing was done out of pressure by fanatical Arabs who had convinced him to do it) both confused and amazed the young Palestinian. These two accounts reveal the other side of Israel, a description of the occasions of Israel's amazing conscience. But the story of highranking military people in Israel attempting a coup to overthrow the government is not well known if known at all. I read a very brief account of this incident in an article about a man called "K", a former head of Mossad. He was the one who had foiled the plot to change the Israeli government, recounted in Time magazine.

The fact is that during both the first and second Intifadas, Israeli military prisons, "brigs" were filled with men who refused to continue to participate in the occupation. Several reports on this subject appeared in the Time magazine I read. But this still was not a well-known fact in the west, and particularly in the United States. Also reported was the amount of Israeli men in therapy in Israel at the time of the Intifadas, suffering themselves, from the psychological damage of carrying out military orders designed to "quell" the Palestinian rebellions. This included indiscriminate "round-ups" of all Palestinian young men over the age of eighteen in any given village, holding them in detention, often torturing them, and, in some cases suddenly releasing them, back into their own villages, in a state of disorientation and physical injury, and trauma.

What Israel faces is the ignominy of a "blanket" racism draped across its whole society; the subjugation of the non-Jewish and indigenous population of historic Palestine. This attitude which permeates all aspects of Israeli society, is to be actually, constantly, breathing in -- a kind of "toxicity" -- only this toxicity is far worse than air pollution which can be brought under control by proper regulations put in place. It is getting inside people's heads and reordering their core ideas about Arab people and the Israelis' relationship to them that is much more difficult to change. To transform people's hearts, to get Israelis to see "straight" on the issue of their relationship to Palestinians, is the crucible Israel rests on.

CHAPTER 12

While asking directions for the bus to Tel Aviv near the Old City in Jerusalem, I chanced to speak to a young Palestinian guy who told me his story about being taken in for questioning by Israeli police, for no apparent reason. Fayad, (not his real name) said that he was detained and questioned by the IDF who apparently suspected him of ties to Palestinian groups who Israeli believes directly threatens their state. Finally, after signing a confession, still he was detained for one year. He was allowed to study in prison in an apparent concession by the Israelis. Upon his release he went back to his shop in the Old City and continued to work. I noticed that Fayad walked with a limp. I did not want to ask him about it as I had a feeling he probably incurred his injury by the IDF who beat him badly during his detention. Speaking with Fayad, I experienced the same sad feeling, I saw people suffering for no reason except that they resent a foreign power occupying their land, Palestine, and occasionally attempt means to remedy their situation.

The Israeli Declaration of Independence is based on secularism but there is a high ambivalence in Israel in this regard. Although many Israelis are not actively religious they continue to have strong feelings about their connection to Judaism. For example, on Shabbat everything is completely shut down and most Israelis obverse it even though many complain that they cannot use the public transport for twenty four hours. While I continued speaking with Fayad, a man who was obviously an orthodox Jew from the way he dressed, moved swiftly past us through the Saturday (Shabbat) crowd of people. I saw that this man noticeably placed what appeared to be a tea towel across his entire face.

"Did you see that?" Fayad asked. "Yes", I answered. And then I asked Fayad why on earth this man was walking around with a kitchen towel wrapped around his face. "It is because it is the Jewish holy day and it is forbidden for an orthodox Jew to look at any gentile or non-Jew". So if an orthodox Jew is required for reasons of any personal emergency to leave the conclave of his community, he has to completely cover his face. I wondered how this man could see to navigate his way through the busy and narrow street.

I will never forget sitting in a restaurant with a friend who was serving as a volunteer in a Palestinian outreach program in East Jerusalem on a Sunday afternoon in Ramallah. It was very crowded with many people having Sunday lunch. The man sitting next to us with his family, obviously the father of the brood with him, in a very polite way asked us, my friend and I, if we were from Israel. "No", my friend gasped in horror. And I then explained we were both Americans, I now living in Mallorca and traveling in the area and that my friend worked in a community program in St. George's Cathedral. Never, ever in my life have I been shown such deference and respect as I was that day by this Palestinian man. It is impossible to describe the kindness and regard in his manner and voice.

As we spoke briefly I could not recall ever in my life being treated with such utmost respect. The man exhibited to me such humility that is very difficult to now describe. I honestly don't think that our culture in the west is capable of producing such true civility. I know there are reports of people being blown up in cafes in the West Bank by terrorists and I don't doubt that these reports are true. But I can only say what happened to me that day, obviously. I experienced the absolute opposite.

My friend, whose name is Polly, said that she couldn't discuss the Middle East and her experiences there with her family anymore. They did not believe her. She said ominously, "the Israelis leave no witnesses" (she was referring to criminal acts committed by Israel). One day she came into the church where she volunteered and lived, to find the kitchen help, comprised largely of Palestinians coming in from the West Bank where they live, waiting for the dishwasher who hadn't yet arrived for his shift. Two hours later he finally arrived and tried to start work for the day. He appeared dazed and in shock. The other kitchen help and Polly asked him to sit down and explain what happened to him and why he was late. Obviously something was wrong. Without saying anything more, the man pulled up his pant legs and shirt. On the back of his legs as well as his back, were huge purple welts. He had been beaten by the police at the usual checkpoint where he came in every day to his job. No one knew why. His papers were in order and he was known to be passing from the West Bank to Israel to work in Jerusalem. He had been detained at the checkpoint for two hours and beaten for no reason. It is noted by human rights organizations that there are members of the IDF who hate Palestinians coming in to work in Israel and will do anything to try to dissuade them from entering Israel on a daily basis even though the economy of the West Bank does not provide anything close to a job market due to the Israeli occupation.

CHAPTER 13

On another occasion upon entering Israel, I was greeted in immigration by a young Israeli woman, who appeared to be the loveliest person and I am sure she was. As she looked through my belongings, we fell into a discussion about the military in Israeli and she proudly said the military in Israel was compelled to follow military standards of the highest ethics. And I did remember meeting the really, absolutely nicest young man sitting next me on the bus, who spoke of his time in the ID, the first time I was in Israel. There was no doubt in my mind that he was the kind of person who would think twice about committed any brutal act. Referring again to the account in Time magazine of how, during the second intifada, Israeli military prisons were filled up with soldiers who would rather face months in "the brig", military prison, than continue to work as soldiers and be ordered and forced to commit horrible acts of violence and terror against Palestinians. And during the first intifada the schedules of Israeli psychologists were filled with Israeli soldiers going through crises because of the horrible things their military superiors were asking them to do on a daily basis.

I was sitting in a dentist's office in Turkey when I chanced to strike up a conversation with a Norwegian man sitting opposite me in the waiting room. The conversation drifted into a subject on the Middle East and as I referred to the human rights violations, he said to me, that the Bible records God himself giving the Jews the land of Israel in perpetuity. Angrily, I exclaimed, "the Jews wrote the Bible so they could write what they wanted". The man was deeply shocked at what I said. I got the impression he could not believe anyone could think that what was in the Bible was anything other than "God's Word". The conversation abruptly ended. Later, I reflected that what I had said might have had vaguely racist undertones. As I exited the dentist's office after my appt. I noticed him sitting silently and still, it seemed to me with a shocked expression on his face as he glanced at me. I wanted to speak to him again and explain my position on the Middle East more fully; what I had seen and heard on my visits there. And explain about the terrible things I now know the Israeli government is responsible for. But I could see from the expression on his face that further conversation would not be welcome.

It is incredible to me that so many "Christians" in the west, or Evangelical Christians so unequivocally support Israel and ignore the plight of the Christian Palestinians. I was introduced to the president of the Bethlehem Bible College on one of my stays in the region, Bashir Awad. He told me in no uncertain terms how the Israeli government created a nightmare in their lives. Even when they need something as simple as having a coca- cola machine installed on their premises, the company takes forever to do so, causing many delays and unnecessary problems and expense for such a simple request. After speaking to Mr. Awad and attending one of the college's services, I could see that doctrinally, his Bible College, was exactly the same as all other Evangelicals in the States. And yet, the needs of the faculty and staff of Bethlehem Bible College, which appear to be dire, are ignored by people in the United States who have great influence on Israel and its policies. One Palestinian man visiting and speaking in a Baptist church in the U.S. was stunned to hear a member of the church ask him how he became a Christian. The man, amazed, in his reply, reminded his co-religionist that Christianity was born in his country, Palestine. Even then, the American had trouble assimilating this information which appeared to be new to him.

A friend of mine in Mallorca told me how she knew someone who had become part of the U.N. peacekeeping force and was sent to the West Bank. When he first arrived he had no particularly strong convictions politically. But when he left the region he said he was totally pro-Palestinian and cited the IDF, under directions of the Israeli government, to be in violation of Palestinian rights. He said he witnessed Israeli soldiers walking unannounced into Palestinian homes, going straight into their kitchens, grabbing whatever was at hand, often a large container of flour and dumping the contents all over the floor. The peacekeeper said that he observed continually the IDF making the lives of the Palestinians as hellish as possible, in an attempt to drive the Palestinians away, out of their homes in the West Bank, I think the events just described were in Hebron, so that Israel could move in and occupy as much of the West Bank as possible.

CHAPTER 14

I was watching Press TV, an international channel in English from Tehran. Appearing on Press TV, are many writers, journalists and academics from the west who cannot report on western channels due to policy restrictions on revealing to the public the often severe crises caused by the American foreign policy and Israel's as well. I watched a report of a Gazan journalist, a man who publicly espoused non-violence, returning to Gaza after receiving a prestigious journalistic award from the Dutch government. He was detained upon arrival in Gaza City by Israeli soldiers who beat him up so severely he had to be hospitalized. The man even sustained a huge red mark on his neck as the result of an Israeli soldier standing on his neck while beating him at the same time. The Israelis kept asking him why, since he was allowed out of Gaza, he wanted to come back. The man explained over and over that he was returning to his family and home in Gaza, a fact which the Israelis found impossible to understand.

Such a report would never be broadcast on ABC, CBS or NBC, American channels. Perhaps on CNN or BBC, and even rarely on those channels, would there be reports revealing the extent of Israeli police brutality.

While spending a day in Gaza, I was taken to the Islamic university. Upon entry I was taken to the women's section and requested to put on a long coat and hijab or scarf covering my whole head. Since the whole area was air-conditioned, it presented no problem to consent to do so. I was introduced to the woman who was the head of the women's dept. She was a lady from Malaysia, I found out, and simply wore what looked like a little white doily on top of her head. There were about nine young women sitting in her study with her. They all looked up as I was brought in to meet them, with great amazement. I was warmly greeted by the President sitting there, as they quietly and respectfully listened to me tell them how lucky I felt to be able to visit Gaza that day and how kind they were to meet with me.

Again, I was treated to a combination of great surprise and true kindness at my desire to come and visit with them. They young ladies were truly taken aback, and although the President could speak English as well as my guide that day, who was a student there herself, I don't think the others present in the room understood much of our exchange. I really felt as warmly received by the President and the others present in her office as it was possible to feel.

After viewing the "state of the art" huge lecture rooms, all brand new and complete with microphones and headsets, we came, my guide and I, and sat in an outdoor garden area. I looked around me at the billboards of all the banks from all the Arab countries in the region who had contributed to the university. There was not one bank listed from the U.S. to assist in the education of young Gazans, certainly not from Israel, or for that matter, anywhere else in the world outside all the Arab countries shown in the billboards all around me.

That, I thought as I sat next to the lady who was my guide, is a truly sad statement, that Gaza and that the Arab world stand alone, without recognition and badly needed support from other banking institutions from all other parts of the world.

CHAPTER 15

It is mysterious than the United States is the only country where nonJews widely practice circumcision on baby boys. There has been a group, mostly considered eccentric, called "The British Israelites" who believe that Britain and also the United States were actually part of the ten lost tribes of Israel. It is amazing to note that both the Balfour Paper and the White Paper originated in the British Parliament. Both documents stressed the now widely considered racist view that the ties of the Jews to the Holy Land were so ancient they superseded the rights of the Arabs. However, the contents of these documents do not reflect the passage in the Bible in Judges Chapter 19, which states that at the time when the legendary King David took control of a city called "Jebus, it was a non-Israelite city", when it became Jerusalem or in Hebrew, Yerushalayim, city of peace. Many Palestinians consider themselves Jebusites or having ancestry that originated in what is now Jerusalem which was at the time the Old Testament book of Judges was written, in fact, Jebus. The Arabs have a very long and complex historical relationship to Jerusalem and to all of Palestine. If examining the history of Palestine objectively, the Arabs roots in Palestine and ancient Canaan are just as deep as that of the descendents of Abraham, Isaac and Jacob, that is the Jews. And in fact, both groups trace their lineage all the back to Abraham and his descendents.

It should be noted in relation to the group calling themselves "British Israelites" that they are considered to have rather contradictory beliefs. The fact is, some of them, such as one of their founders, Edward Hine, were also anti-semitic.

It is also remarkable to note in light of these historical legends, i.e. British and American people being part of the ten Lost Tribes, that it has been the United States which unilaterally and unequivocally has supported the nation of Israel today, although Israel has defied countless UN resolutions demanding change in its policies toward Palestinians and condemning its actions. The United States has stood firmly behind Israel and its refusal to comply with U.N. resolutions. And no matter what human rights violations Israel has committed, this thoroughly confusing position of the U.S. continues to this day.

Many rights activists and political analysts today support the dismantling of Israel's Jewish supremacist position, politically, and as was in the case of South Africa, create a new politic that completely equalizes both Arabs and Jews in the areas of what is known today as Israel proper, the West Bank and Gaza. Though the Gaza has been a separate enclave for centuries with long ties to Egypt, in the Israeli War of Independence in 1948, the Gaza was flooded with refugees fleeing the terrors of war-ridden Palestine. The people of Gaza, which was then a peaceful place and enjoyed a prosperous merchant class, had excellent soil for its extensive agriculture, and a fishing industry stretching from Egypt to Cyprus, were totally bewildered by the the massive influx of population who were expelled from Israel into the West Bank and Gaza.

So from that time the demography of the Gaza was drastically altered to include a large population of former Palestinians who had lived, many for centuries, in western Palestine which in 1948 was declared to be the state of Israel.

The Knesset has some Arab-Israelis holding positions in it, yet without full citizenship, most other Palestinians still remain without the ability to vote, creating a virtually apartheid political situation in Israel. This is obviously the crucial issue, the ability of all Palestinians to vote and to have equal rights to Israelis. And in considering Hamas, although it came to power in Gaza by wide support of the population there, it remains an Islamic theocracy and thus does not qualify, for this reason, as a real democratic government. It should be noted that many are unaware that it was actually Israel who, in the early 1980's created Hamas out of a group of Muslims affiliated with the Muslim Brotherhood in Egypt in the hopes that these ultra religious people would be easier to deal with than Yasser Arafat and the PLO. This idea obviously backfired for the Israelis.

Not long after Hamas took power in Gaza there was a considerable outbreak of violence between them and the Fatah resistance under Arafat. There were deaths and reports of people killing even close relatives, leaving the new government badly damaged in terms of its reputation in the international community.

The Palestinian Authority today under Mahmoud Abbas, attempts to dialogue with all and any Israeli spokespersons, but is soiled by allegations of torture and incarceration of Palestinians who oppose it or disagree with the PA policities. The Amnesty International December 2018 publication of the case of Suha Jbara gives a horrifying account of a peace activist who was beaten and tortured by the PA. Quoting directly from the AI publication is the following. "Suha Jbara is a Palestinian, US and Panamanian citizen and social justice activist involved with Islamic charities. She also works to support the families of Palestinian prisoners in Israel. On 3 November she was arrested during a violent raid on her home. During questioning by prosecutors, she was accused of asked about collecting and distributing money in illegal ways, an accusation she denies.

Palestinian forces in the West Bank and Gaza have a track record of arbitrarily arresting peaceful activists, demonstrators and critics, many of whom have faced judicial proceedings that do not meet fair trial standards."

Certainly, given these facts the effectuation of a solid political change in Israel would point to the dismantling of the three political structures, and one entirely new political assembly, or parliamentary system formed which would be comprised of the many factions of the region and would ensure the rights of all people today in Israel, the West Bank and the Gaza. A solid and honest "unity government", which would, without a doubt, constitute a truly significant political, if not transformational change, in the Middle East.

Another one of the major factors for pushing forward a seriously practical resolution in the region, aside from the dire human rights crisis, is that of opening the groups up to free trade and opportunity for business between the two communities. There are often allegations of Israelis selling cars to Palestinians which is illegal under Israeli law. There are widespread allegations of Israelis actually selling arms to Palestinians, even to Gaza. The government of Israel, of course, vigorously denies that these allegations are true. But according to some reports, it would appear that some Israelis go to any lengths to increase their income. An all inclusive political resolution would bring an end to such a scurrilous black market between Israel and Palestinians. The situation is one that highlights the tremendous need for financial trade to open up and be made legal between Israel and the West Bank and Gaza.

CHAPTER 16

In recent public remarks the current Presidential Candidate, himself from a Jewish background, Bernie Sanders, has condemned in no uncertain language the disproportionate numbers of Palestinians murdered, tortured and injured by Israeli governmental and military forces in the constant conflict in the occupied territories, most recently occurring in the Israeli attacks on Gaza in the summer of 2014. His remarks to the press, go farther in condemning Israel's military policies in the occupied territories than any other prominent American politician. His allegations are backed by Amnesty International and B'Tselem and even the U.S. State Dept. His support of Palestinian human rights are desperately needed by the people he wants to support and do not go unnoticed by human rights advocates inside the U.S. who can vote him into power, as well as among concerned Israelis who protest the ruthless policies of Israel. His remarks can be read in an online publication, "Salon", April 22, of this year. Bernie Sanders has made a proposal to introduce into the Democratic Party's platform on policy toward Israel, a statement to ensure the protection, both legal and ethical, of Palestinian rights.

Israeli society is often accused of practicing racist and discriminatory policies in terms of housing, personal attitudes and other institutional situations where racism is accused by minorities (Jews of color) as being all too present. The forty percent of european, North American, Ashkenazi Jews who dominate and essentially control the policies and politics of Israeli society are frequently under attack for practicing racist policies to Ethiopian Jews and to Jews of non-european and Arab backgrounds. Many Ethiopian Jews, for example allege experiencing racism in their daily lives in Israel. Israel's Ashkenazis cite a huge culture gap that is the reason for divisions among them. For example, on seeing TV for the first time showing a movie depicted a burning house, an elderly Ethiopian woman grabbed a broom and smashed the TV. She explained that she was trying to put out the fire, fearing it would enter the home she was in. Many Ethiopians feel that Ashkenazi Jews believe they are superior to Ethiopians and other Jews of color inside Israel, as well.

Even though Israel launched "Operations Moses and Solomon to rescue Falasha or Ethiopian Jews in 1984, many Ethiopians reported to authorities they encountered seriously long delays in receiving immigration papers and enjoying full rights under Israeli law. Israel responded by claiming that the Jewish authenticity of Ethiopians remained under question and claimed the need for further studies, even though, the government had already rescued the very people who, apparently, they questioned were Jews.

In spite of the negative portrayals of Arabs in childrens' schoolbooks as primitive farmers or terrorists, it is important to realize that for example, there is a network of bilingual schools. "Hand in Hand" in Israel, has six schools to date and is conducted by teachers that are both Israeli and Palestinian. This group struggles to promote understanding and equality between the two groups in Israel.

While it is critical to recognize the valiant efforts of Hand in Hand and other like-minded peace organizations in Israel, these efforts are overshadowed by what can be seen on a video produced by Jewish Voice for Peace interviewing a Palestinian mother whose little boy never came home from school. Later she found out her child was shot by Israeli soldiers. Palestinian people are still engulfed in nightmares such as the previous account. The bilingual schools are helpful, to be sure, in making a connection at least at the educational level among Jews and Arabs, but are still only "cosmetic". Israel desperately needs real and substantial structural change in its government that will provide equal democratic rights to the entire population of the region, fully including Palestinians. Israel has to stop being known as a democracy for Jews only.

Israel is a society made up of people riven by wildly divergent ideas and values. When Baruch Goldman, the fanatic Jewish West Bank settler, murdered thirty Muslims at prayer in Abraham's Tomb in 1994, a report was issued from the West Bank interviewing residents of the Hebron area as to their responses to this incident. One Jewish woman, with real pain in her voice said, "innocent people died". While another Israeli man said, "so what", or words to the effect that he didn't care if someone murdered thirty Arabs. Maybe he was even glad it happened, such was the impression the viewer had.

Regarding the unusually close connection of the U.S. to Israel, many Arabs make the comment that Israel is the 53rd state of the U.S. On a flight to Tel Aviv, the elderly Israeli man sitting next to me said, referring to the U.S. "they own us". The U.S, certainly plays a dominant role in determining Israeli policy and for this reason it would appear that not all Israelis view the U.S. favorably. Secretly and as I experienced, openly, some Israelis resent what is viewed as U.S. political dominance over their country.

CHAPTER 17

One of the most difficult issues to address is the issue of the womens' dress code prevalent among Muslims. No matter how hot the weather, Muslim women are compelled by current religious dictates to cover absolutely every hair on their heads with elastic bands and scarves and from head to foot wear coats of heavy winter-like material to cover and disguise any conceivable curve of a woman's body. To a western observer and, in fact to some women in the Arab and Muslim world as well, this practice is unbelievable and unconscionable. And extremely difficult to bear, to say the least, in a hot climate. Any comment on the hardship this presents to women is taken to be anti-Muslim and prejudiced against their beliefs. I remember speaking to an Italian woman who said she had traveled in the West Bank twenty years prior to when I was traveling in the region which was in the 1990's. So the period of time she referred to was in the 1970's. She said woman dressed normally, without headscarves that cover the entire throat and hair, and without such heavy clothing all during the hot season.

I recall while on my way to visit the West Bank one afternoon, sitting next to a lady, who told me she was Christian. In a soft-spoken way she quietly pointed out to me the Muslim women on the bus who were covered from head to toe. This lady, who was dressed in a regular summer dress, although a conservative style, told me that, "this started about six years ago. Before that, Muslim women dressed much like all the other women of Palestine, only wearing a small scarf on top of their heads", similar to the "doily" I had seen on the head of the president of the women's section at the Islamic University in Gaza, I thought as I listened to this lady.

Apparently, the revolution in Iran, where women began their head to toe dress, or so I surmised, had affected the rest of the Islamic community. It is said that an ultra extremist Islamic sect, the Wahhabists, or Wahhabism, originating in Saudi Arabia, had been the influence on Islam that brought about the extreme dress now seen among so many Muslim women, in predominantly Muslim countries. In Turkey, for example, many Turkish women are completely shocked and confused that such a "backlash of medieval dress" has affected so many women in their country, as well.

It is mind boggling to see that, although the United States foreign policy does not seem to have the same good will toward Arab countries', that other countries enjoy, it is, in fact, in the

United States that finally a much needed reform movement inside Islam, has begun. Hopefully, this freedom will spread around the world and into the Islamic Community, or "Omah", which is the worldwide body of Islamic believers.

Continuing on this subject, I viewed on TV recently a Muslim man now living in the U.S. who stated that though it is a small portion still, of Islam, there are mosques who do not practice gender segregation. The women and men sit together in the service just as in Christian services and in synagogues. And among these Muslims, women dress normally, appropriate to the weather. I have often reflected that the extreme dress adopted recently by the women of Islam is an attempt to remove themselves as far as possible from anything to do with the west or western values. Hopefully this attitude will change in other parts of the world as well, as many Muslims do, in fact, believe Muslims traditions need to be reexamined and very likely, reformed.

CHAPTER 18

The irony is that Jewish people are safer anywhere else in the world than in Israel. The whole reason for the state of Israel to be created or "resurrected" from its ancient history, was that at last Jews would be safe from horrors such as the holocaust which occurred under the Third Reich, during the Second World War. But having an army to defend them and a state based primarily on their ethnicity alone has actually created more horrors than they ever imagined being subjected to, when the state of Israel began in 1948. The refusal on the part of Israel to acknowledge that Palestine was densely populated and that the modern Israeli state is based on a theft of another country is the root of the ongoing controversy surrounding Palestinian rights. Palestine, although never a sovereign state, had been part of several empires for 2,000 years since the fall of Rome, and had a very long history which included Jews. The current state of Israel adopted, to a very large degree, the idea that Palestine had very little history in the past 2,000 years. As was just pointed out, this was untrue. Palestine had been part of the Byzantine Empire, then the Caliphates of Baghdad and Damascus, and finally the Ottoman Empire just prior to the British Mandate. There had been a kind of congress or parliament in Constantinople that met once a year during the Ottoman Empires. Palestine, although a small region, had been considered important enough to have two delegates present at annual parliaments.

The greatest density of Jewish population is found in the United States, the second largest Jewish population, incredibly enough, in Germany.

This is followed by France, which holds the third greatest Jewish population in the world. In the U.S. Jews are integrated completely throughout society and in every way enjoy normal and productive lives. In European countries, there are incidences of racist attacks against synagogues and other racist attacks but a case could be made that Jewish lives are still far safer in Germany, France or any other European country than living in Israel. The lives of Israelis are seriously and constantly threatened by mandatorily having to serve in the military plus having to constantly worry about attacks by Palestinians who have suffered egregious deprivations under Israeli occupation.

It is also true that Israel sought a much greater area of land. This was pointed out to me by a Palestinian activist who showed me and several others in a tour of Ramallah, an Israeli coin.

Holding up the coin so we could all see it, he pointed to a land mass on the coin which he said was actually representing all of Palestine, the Sinai, part of Iraq and Syria, as well as Lebanon. This was the greater Israel that Ariel Sharon and even David Ben Gurion had once espoused as a full and complete Jewish state.

CHAPTER 19

An Israeli friend told me that Israelis are constantly spying on each other and that there are other spies, spying on the spies, in a long chain of people spying on each other. He told me there is very little trust among Israelis. Something of an understatement when one considers the long chain of spying among Israelis so described.

I recall sitting in a cafe in the heart of the labyrinthian streets of Old Jerusalem. A Jewish man (he wore a yamaka, the hat of an orthodox Jew) walked in and asked for either some food or something I could not quite hear. The Arab waiter in the cafe smiled, almost stood at attention and quickly complied with the Israeli's request. After which the Israeli turned, and crossing the narrow street, could be observed taking a large key out of his pocket and pressing it into a door in a wall that looked like it had not been opened in years, the Israeli disappeared inside.

On another occasion I saw two young men both in their early twenties walking together outside Damascus Gate in an animated and happy conversation. One youth, was wearing distinctly Arab dress, a long robe with the fez on his head, and the other wore the heavy suit and yamika of an orthodox Jew. The relationships of people living together in what can only be termed as historic Palestine are often mind-boggling.

While staying in a hostel in West Jerusalem which was part of a Methodist Church and staffed by both Israelis and Palestinians, I spoke to a man from the states who was a writer. He said he had been in the West Bank when the first intifada took place. He witnessed an Israeli soldier shoot a boy of about ten years old point blank in the face, and saw the boy die on the spot. When the writer asked the soldier in shocked tones how he could murder a child, the Israeli shrugged and said it was part of war. When he was reminded of the Geneva Conventions which certainly prohibit the murder of children, the soldier simply walked away and wouldn't speak anymore. Just walked away.

A numbing feeling of helplessness spread through me. How many people in the west have ever heard a story like this about Israel who is almost always presented as a victim in the media?

CHAPTER 20

I wanted to see the ancient tunnels underneath Old Jerusalem just before they closed to tourist passage, at noon. I walked down at around 11:30 to the entrance where I saw, about twenty feet in front of me, an absolutely movie-like scenario. Two Israeli soldiers were rushing out of the tunnel entrance, their uzi machine guns, lifted in the air and at the ready. I was informed that the tunnel was closing early and I had to leave. I realized then in the most visceral and visual way that I was in the middle of a perpetual war zone.

It was in Old Jerusalem as well, not far from the Jewish quarter, atop a small hill over the Via Dolorosa which is in the Arab quarter, that three little children, all, holding hands, skipped up to me. Smiling and laughing, there was a light in the little boy's eyes that was unusual and so magical. The look in the little boy's eyes was truly something I honestly had never seen before. The happiness and the joy and power in the child's eyes and the absolute merriment exuded by the two little girls as well, was overwhelming. It was as though angels suddenly possessed the bodies of these dear little children and gave me the most beautiful message direct from Heaven . . . A message of a celestial future free of the horrors that presently encompass the Holy Land. I will never forget it. The message of love and power shining out of the childrens' eyes told me of a world so wonderful it cannot be imagined. I felt like the tiny emissaries had emerged from the very walls of the Old City, that they had been part of it for centuries, were living fragments of the ancient stones themselves, and that they had suddenly come to life like a wonderful fairy tale . . .

In Jerusalem the Israelis have created the famous Yad Vashem, the holocaust memorial. A very nice lady who lived part of the year in Israel and the other in Canada, asked me if I had been to visit the memorial. I told her "no", that I knew all about the Nazi horrors and did not wish to see them recounted again. "It is so disturbing", I explained. On numerous occasions I reflected how, so many Israelis were so caught up still in the memory of the Third Reich and its cruel destruction of so many Jews as well as many non- Jews. At times it seemed to me that Yad Vashem existed, on an unconscious level, as a kind of justification for the necessity of occupying Palestine and the resulting suffering and complete disenfranchisement of so many Palestinians. In a stange and terrible way the Holocaust Memorial seemed to be a celebration of the holocaust and the Nazis. Because so many in Israel believed that without the holocaust they never could have established the Jewish state in Palestine.

I read of a guide taking visitors through the Memorial who overheard a conversation among Israelis. There was a group of young Israelis, all in uniform, visiting the Memorial, accompanied by their commanding officer, that day. The guide overheard a young soldier make the following remark to his CO. Upon reading in a plaque over the entrance of how Jews were displaced in various eastern European countries during the 1700's, the young officer exclaimed to his Israeli C.O., "But that is just what we are doing now to the Palestinians". The next time the guide visited with another group of visitors, he noticed immediately that the plaque regarding Jewish displacement in Europe had been removed.

Many times during my visit to Israel and the region, I thought about Abraham, who is considered to be the very father of the Jews, the great patriarch of the Christian faith, and the father of Islam as well. The Bible accounts how Abraham always deferred. In the book of Genesis, when he and his nephew Lot, decided to not continue to journey together, and part ways, Abraham, giving first choice to Lot, asked Lot which way he would choose. Lot looked down at the green, well watered agriculturally developed great civilizations of Sodom and Gomorrah, and decided that moving in the direction of those cities looked like the best path to take. Abraham agreed and took his flocks, family members and all his goods into the Rocky Mountains above where they stood. He chose the rocky, unforgiving terrain where water appeared to be scarce. Yet Abraham prospered while Lot did not. Most people know the story of fire and brimstone raining down on the cities Lot choose and how narrowly he and his family were able to escape the doomed cities. Abraham achieved his success not by pushing but by deferring.

Many years ago I read Maxim Khalil's book, "How Israel Lost Its Soul". Maxim Khalil was a journalist of French-Lebanese background who served in the Labour Party of the Knesset in the early 1960's. In his book he tells the story of a wealthy and influential Dutch Jew, who, taking a great interest in the new state of Israel in the 1950's, went to Israel and began to speak with numerous Arab leaders and Arab officials. This man then informed the Israeli government that he found many Arab leaders very open to peace and to working together to make two states, existing peacefully side by side and mutually open to trade and finance. Suddenly the Dutchman was dead. Mr. Khalil had information that he had been murdered by Mossad. When he went to the newspapers with his reports in Israel, he was suddenly arrested and thrown in jail on phony, trumped up charges. Eventually Khalil was released but forced to leave Israel as he believed he would no longer be safe there.

I have wondered so often after watching reports on TV about the current nightmares in the Middle East and likened these reports to what would have been the world's reaction if, during the holocaust, reporters at the end of each day had toured the death camps, reported the dead, reported the mindless atrocities committed and then finished their reports and went home having completed their job for the day, the Third Reich continuing on with its daily horrors unabated. I can't help but wonder how it is any different with the reports from the region recounting endlessly violations of Israelis against Palestinians, which reports continue to this very day.

In the same book, by Khalil, an account is given of a young man working closely with Chaim Weizmann, a physician and the second great architect of the Zionist movement. The actual founder of zionism was Theodor Herzl, a Jewish Austrian newspaperman. One morning this young man came running into the office of Weissman, in a terrible state. "We are doing a great injustice here", he told Weissman. The young man went on to say that Palestine was not a sparsely populated country, an idea promoted by the Zionists, their slogan being "a land without people for a people without a land", but was in fact, very densely populated. In fact the assistant working toward creating a Jewish state on the actual land mass in Palestine that was supposed to be virtually unoccupied, showed that such an empty land mass simply did not exist. Yet, Weissman, calmed his assistant down and somehow convinced him that the Jewish cause for a homeland was so legitimate that the removal or displacement of some Palestinian communities would prove to be thoroughly justified. Weissman still seemed to believe an unpopulated area in Palestine existed, if they just continued to study the area carefully enough. In the end of their struggle for a Jewish state, it was to be over 1,000,000 Palestinian Arabs displaced. Although the official figure given by Israel is 700,000. The figures of Arabs who lost their homes and properties and lives in Palestine is still a subject of much dispute.

CHAPTER 21

On my way back from a visit into the West Bank, I was stopped in a group taxi by the Israeli soldiers at the checkpoint to enter Israel. The two young guys looked at me and almost appeared to laugh. Casually they brushed my passport which I had opened to them, aside. However, two very pleasant looking young Palestinian men were told in clipped tones that they had to stand aside, they could not enter Israel yet.

Here I was, an American citizen from so very far away, being allowed to enter Israel without the slightest problem and because I was an American. Yet two young people whose ancestors had lived in Palestine for centuries were being subjected to possibly big problems in order to enter what was very possibly their workplace.

I read an article some time ago in a magazine such as the New Yorker or Atlantic Monthly, about a discussion taking place between a traveling American and two young Arab boys. The American asked the boys where they had been born. They told him the name of a village that the American, touring Israel had never heard of in his travels. He eventually discovered that the village where the boys had been born had been razed to the ground and no longer existed because the Ben Gurion airport stood in its place. The feeling the man conveyed in his writing as he told this story was that the village had no right to have been there in the first place and that the boys had no right to have been born there. Apparently, it was absolutely unreal to this Jewish American that these Arab boys could clearly remember and recount their lives as they grew up in the village of their birth, until it was destroyed in order to build the Gurion airport.

CHAPTER 22

When Israel bombed Gaza in December of 2008 and January 2009, and the whole world protested the slaughter of the civilian population, and although Israel prohibited journalists from reporting, reports did come later of scenes of bodies of young children splattered all over the streets of Gaza City, I began to pass out flyers to the many tourists visiting Alanya, Turkey where I lived. In these flyers I quoted 1,400 Gazans were killed 350 of which were children and almost all of these were civilians. These figures I obtained from Press TV, an international TV station broadcasting from Tehran and London. I asked the people to write to their heads of state and demand that their countries break diplomatic ties with Israel.

As I handed flyers to a group of young women from Russia in a busy outdoor market, one girl just glanced at the flyer and practically burst into tears. She was the only one to react to my account of the carnage presently visited on a civilian population and leaving so many dead and gravely injured. Even doctors tending to the wounded in and around ambulances were shot at by Israeli jets overhead. One doctor lost both legs. The Russian girl remarked how Tzipi Livni, a prominent Israeli politician who supported these military attacks on Gaza, where these nightmares were occurring was a woman with children of her own. How weak is the human conscience in the face of nationalism. The most unthinkable cruelties and injustices are blindly and blankly accepted in the name of Jewish nationalism.

Journalists reporting from Gaza during and after the 2008-2009 attacks told of having headaches that continued after leaving the region. Israel used DP bombs, which is depleted plutonium. These bombs are more radioactive than the bombs used on the civilian population in Nagasaki, Japan, during the Second World War. Scientists say that eventually the whole poisonous and lethal cloud of toxicity will eventually waft over Israel. While thirteen Israelis died in these attacks on Gaza over 1,400 Gazans died, the vast majority being civilians and children. There were some Gazans who had armed themselves and attempted to repel Israeli attacks. According to Wikipedia, Israel claims its attacks were in response to the Gazan government's continued attacks against Israeli cities with rudimentary, "homemade" bombs.

The news channels in the west, CNN, BBC and others gave scant coverage of "Operation Cast Lead". However, the horrific slaughter of so many civilians and children was considered critical enough for Press TV to give extensive coverage for three weeks, until the cessation of hostilities.

CHAPTER 23

I think any responsible person of reasonable education, acknowledges the unique and amazing contribution to science, cultural development and humanism by Jews in the west. Jews are credited with creating the whole concept of ethics. I remember speaking to a friend, not particularly well informed politically, who said in absolute wonder, in reaction to Israel's policies, "the Jews of all people".

And I reflected on a fragment of the conversation I had with Polly, working at St. George's Church in east Jerusalem, "the Israelis leave no witnesses". A really ominous statement.

My oldest sister married an Arab-American. Their two children, my niece and nephew, are the prototypes of Jewish people, who are often characterized as wealthy and highly educated. The fact is my nephew became extremely successful in a business creating high tech communications systems and my niece became the head of all the school districts of a large American city. They are often mistaken for being Jewish. I spoke with a Jewish friend who made the remark, "there is barely any difference between an Arab and a Jew".

While on a tour of Ramallah the Palestinian guide told me that on a remote mountain, called Mt. Gerizim above Nablus, a large West Bank town, lived the Samaritan Jews, probably the oldest remnant of the Jewish people. They have a book, an ancient text, they believe was written by Aaron, the brother of Moses that they read from, in their synagogue, once a year. The members of this community do not have Israeli citizenship, as some Palestinians do. It is reported that one of their rabbis was even a member of one of the outer circles of the PLO. (The former PLO had several inner and outer circles of members). The Palestinian guide said that the Samaritan Jews speak a form of Hebrew so ancient that there is hardly any difference at all between what they speak, and the Arabic spoken today throughout the Arab world.

When Desmond Tutu visited Gaza City he told the media interviewing him that what he witnessed in Gaza was worse than any horror he had seen in the townships in the worse days of apartheid.

CHAPTER 24

When I read Golda Meir's autobiography, I was struck with the statement she made that she wanted to "put pay to the false allegation" that the Israeli Army or Haganah in 1948 stole land from the Palestinians. Yet, in the same book and almost in the same breath she blandly refers to Palestinians who were "displaced". She gives three different figures of when these displacements occurred. One figure was 235,000, then a figure around 450,000 people, and finally a figure of 600,000. These figures amount to well over 1,000,000 people. These displaced persons, referred to in Meir''s biography were people who were forced to leave their homes, their belongings, and at gun point were forced into the West Bank, or western Palestine, where they had nowhere to live. Golda Meir, a woman of staggering, towering character, who was referred to by Ben Gurian as "the only real man on his cabinet", made the statement, widely accepted at the time, that there "were no Palestinian people". That the people of Palestine roughly identified with the wider Arab world, and that there was no collective, cultural Palestinian identity at all, was an idea promoted by Golda Meir. It was Yassir Arafat, who with his brother, went to Kuwait in the 1960's and the two made their fortunes in oil, that determined to unify and inform Palestinians of their historic identity. Thus becoming a millionaire, Arafat turned his attention to his own people, many of whom were now stateless. With his money and other international donors Arafat established the PLO. Meir claimed that it was he, Arafat, who began the Palestinian movement and that prior to his public declarations to the Arab community in Palestine "we are the Palestinian people", no such identity among the Arabs of Palestine existed.

Palestine, since the fall of the Roman Empire has been part of various empires, as has been mentioned previously. Firstly, the Byzantine Empire ruled from then Constantinople which is now Istanbul in today's Turkey. But with the rise of Islam and the center of the early Christian faith relocating to Rome, Palestine fell under the rule of the caliphate of Baghdad, followed by rule under the caliphate of Damascus. Then Palestine was part of the Ottoman Empire which was followed by the British Mandate and the subsequent endeavors of both Arabs and Jews to create an independent, sovereign state in Palestine.

CHAPTER 25

I have often thought that the modern day Israel represents the shadow and not the substance of the Jewish people. I was in a well-known cafe and restaurant when I lived in Mallorca telling the owner (who told me one of his grandfathers´ was Jewish) and others about my travels in the Middle East. Jeffrey, the owner, exclaimed "Tchouki, how can you go to that country of ethnic cleansing"? I went to some lengths to explain to him that when I visited the region I was traveling in the West Bank as well as Israel and had even been able to visit the Gaza on my last trip. Giving Jeffrey this information quieted him considerably. And shows how false the idea that all Jews support Israel and its policies.

It is shocking to know that when a survey was taken among Americans about the Middle East crisis, the majority actually believed that Arabs occupied Jewish land in Israel, so great is the influence of Israeli propaganda in the United States.

It has been pointed out by psychologists and others that when people suffer trauma for a long time, such as youngsters who suffer abuse growing up, they are likely to become abusers themselves. How often have Palestinians compared their situation since 1948, which they refer to as "Nakba" or the disaster, as the Israelis taking the place of the Nazis and themselves, the Jews. In fact, many Palestinians have been known to refer to themselves as "the new Jews".

Israelis often claim that Israeli citizenship was offered to all the Arabs in Palestine in 1948. However, in the book "O Jerusalem", written by two journalists, Larry Collins and Dominique Lapierre, it is explained that when the Israeli government publicly announced this opportunity to the Arabs, so many came forward to accept the offer and become Israeli citizens, that after 100,00 Arabs received citizenship, the new Jewish government closed the offer. Apparently they had remained unaware of the massive population of Palestinians, as well as the willingness of so many Arabs in Palestine to accept the Zionists and became part of their new state. The fact is, the Israeli government conferred among themselves and realized if they continued to hand out citizenship in their new state, to the indigenous and non-Jewish population of Palestine, Jews would soon be outnumbered. They acknowledged vehemently to each other that a Jewish state as they envisioned, could not exist, if every Arab in Palestine had citizenship in the new state of Israel.

It is, in fact, the west that is responsible for the annihilation of european Jewry in the holocaust. When a secretary on the presidential cabinet was asked by Hitler's Third Reich if the

United States would take into their country the Jews of Germany, the response was "what would we do with all those Jews". Obviously, the United States knew very well that the Jews of Germany and Europe were in deep trouble given the implications of the request from Germany to relocate the Jews of that country into the United States. This account from the history of the Second World War is an implicit indictment of the West in its failure to save millions of lives. The bitterness and shock on the part of so many Jews who were allowed to be decimated by the West, is also implicit in the reckless and shocking disregard for the lives and security of the indigenous population of Palestine. Although in no way responsible for what happened to the Jews of Europe under the Third Reich, inexplicably, the Arabs were the group of people punished for the moral failure of the United States and other countries to protect Jews from the holocaust when they were offered by Germany a way to do so.

In the 1950's the Israeli parliament passed laws prohibiting Palestinians from re-entering Israel from the West Bank to collect the valuables and belongings which they were unable to take with them when forced by Israel to leave their homes, in what became Israel, with only what they could carry. Other Palestinians forcibly relocated into other areas of Israel were also refused entry into the homes and to the premises which they had been living in. All the property including valuables, had been confiscated by the Israelis, or some would say stolen, in order to create their new Jewish state.

In the storyline of John Le Carre's novel, "The Little Drummer Girl", reference is made to Jews in the United States and Europe who by the 1960's had come to decry Israel's statehood because of its conduct toward Palestinians. Inside the plot of this book one older Jewish lady exclaims, "the state of Israel is the destruction of all of Jewish culture and its contribution to the west". The character in the novel continues further saying in no uncertain terms that she believes the creation of Israel has resulted in the death of Jewish culture, its identity, its ethics and its morality.

It is critical to recognize the powerful, comprehensive efforts of academics and writers such as Noam Chomsky, Norman Finkelstein, Miko Peled, Phyllis Bennis, and many other members of the Jewish community, too numerous to name. These people, who have publicly, through their writings and other efforts denounced the racism and injustice of Israel, have paved the path to the restoration of Jewish integrity against the ugly face of the Zionist state.

All of these people, together with dissidents inside Israel and human rights supporters worldwide, believe Israel must be replaced with a modern, secular and democratic state, which would grant full and completely equal political rights for Palestinians as well as Jews.

It is surely difficult to understand why more high-ranking Israelis such as the family of Miko Peled did, refused to countenance the outrageous idea of living in homes that were stolen from so many Palestinian families, forcing them into a state of utter destitution and statelessness. In her own autobiography, Golda Meir writes how foolish and destructive it was to send troops into war and yet there was no question in her mind that it was necessary. She later states that anyone who would think Israel planned to continue to indefinitely occupy the West Bank was "crazy". The occupation of the West Bank was to be short-term, she stated firmly. What would Golda Meir say today?

CHAPTER 26

Another of the worst horror stories to come out of Israel was the death of a young woman, Rachael Kourey from Seattle, Washington who had gone to the Gaza strip to live with Gazans and participate as a human rights worker with the organization founded by an American Jew, Adam Shapiro, as well as others. The movement, known as the International Solidarity Movement, has been pivotal in alleviating the stress and fear of everyday living in Gaza simply by its members living among Gazans to show their support for their struggle to obtain political freedom.

As is common in Gaza, a house was to be scheduled for demolition. This particular demolition happened to be the home of a doctor and his family that Rachel knew. She was a close personal friend of this family and knew and often played with their children.

The fact is, Palestinians in many cases if not most, have lived in their homes and in some cases their ancestors, as well, for sometimes a century, perhaps even longer. Since its inception, the government of Israel can, under their own laws which they make, enter Palestinian towns and reorganize the roads. In this way, Israel makes the Palestinian homes, because of their new location on maps the Israelis themselves have made, now become illegal.

When the bulldozer came to bulldoze down her friends' family home, Rachel sat in front of it and would not move. The driver of the bulldozer, an Israeli soldier, said in the report he made out describing his afternoon's orders of the demolition, that there "had been an object" in the way of the bulldozer. I watched a video of the aftermath of this event when Rachel Kourey had been taken to the famous Al-Shifa Hospital in Gaza City, and pronounced dead. The weeping and screaming of the doctor's son who had known Rachael well, was so heart-breaking that it is impossible to ever, ever forget. I have never heard any weeping, any sorrow expressed as what I heard and saw on this video. Never.

At her funeral, a large Israeli tank came right up to the grave and to the mourners. Spitting out smoke, gunning its engine, the driver of the tank made the most horrible and loud noises as he could. As if the hatred of the Israeli soldiers in taking the life of this unbelievably brave young woman were not enough, whoever these Israelis were, they were compelled to show as much disrespect and hatred as possible at her graveside where stood her parents who had flown all the way from the west coast of the U.S., and dear friends and co-workers in Gaza, commemorating her precious life.

It should be noted, as well, that many Palestinian lives have been lost in the conflict and that they do not often bring the notoriety of the case of Rachel Kourey into the international press, who went into Gaza, which is actually a war zone, as an international helper or rights worker. It is often pointed out by Palestinian activists and other rights supporters that nonwestern people of other color and faith do not receive the same concern as people from the West who are injured or as a result of their rights and support activity in the region of Palestine even lose their lives as Rachel Kourey did. It is critical to remember than many Palestinians are struggling for the simple right of security of person (that they will not be attacked or murdered in their own homes) to this day.

Later, journalists friendly to Israel printed articles that were lies about Rachel Kourey, saying that she had been in underground tunnels helping transport arms into Gaza, when the tunnel collapsed. But by then the story of Rachel Kourey and her death at the hands of the Israeli-driven bulldozer had been widely published and few believed these fallacious reports.

The parents of Rachel Kourey applied for help, asking then President George W. Bush to demand of the government of Israel an inquiry into the entire incident and bring to justice the man who had murdered their daughter. President Bush declined to assist the family in any way to bring the man responsible for Rachel Kourey's death, (cold-blooded murder) to justice.

Not long after the death of Rachel Kourey there were reports in the media of John Deere and Caterpillar, well-known companies that make bulldozers and have good business importing them to Israel, being attacked by the Presbyterian Church, USA and Human Rights Watch based in New York State. These two organizations, seeking justice for Palestinians, are highlighting the death of Rachel Kourey, as well as many other Palestinians who lost their homes and were injured by Israeli soldiers. It remains unclear whether these two companies have actually ceased the business of their companies with Israel or simply have taken significant heat in the press, from official media reports from religious and human rights organizations for selling bulldozers to Israel in what amounts to criminal usage in the occupied territories. That is, as shown, destroying Palestine homes and agriculture as well as injuring and murdering resistant homeowners and human rights workers.

For many years Israel tried to cover up the massacres at Deir Yassin, the Arab village in the West Bank, which occurred in April, 1948. In Ben Gurion's diary, he records disavowing all knowledge of the incident after receiving a letter from King Abdullah of Jordan, the grandfather of the current King of that country. Nazi-like atrocities were committed by a group of Jews who refused to identify themselves. It is generally thought they were a group like the Stern Gang, if not the Stern Gang themselves who were responsible for disemboweling pregnant women, ripping earrings out of the ears of Palestinian women, subjecting them to other injuries, and then raping them. In one instance, a young woman ran after an old man and murdered him with an ax. The survivors, including small terrified children were then paraded in a truck through Jerusalem before being executed somewhere outside that city. The Irgun, out of which the Stern Gang had emerged, was an outlawed army, unlike the Haganah, which was headed by Ben Gurion and considered by Israel to be its legitimate army. Later, the Haganah became the IDF or Israeli Defense Forces. However, the Irgun practiced terrorism throughout the West Bank before and during the 1950′s.

The story of the massacres in Deir Yassin in 1948 are recounted in "O Jerusalem", a book detailing events surrounding the inception of Israel, referred to earlier. What occurred at Deir Yassin is also recorded in the files of the Red Cross which had many medical workers in Palestine at that time. It is now reported in the Israeli media itself that the Irgun indiscriminately attacked Arabs in their villages, murdering many. They succeeded in inciting enough terror to cause many Arab families to flee the region entirely.

I read in the 1990′s an article in Time magazine. Living in a remote area of Mallorca, I read every word in the magazine which I subscribed to. As I turned the page of the magazine one day, my eye fell on an article about Israel. There was a photograph of a young woman dressed a bit unconventionally which reminded me of the ′60′s and the countercultural movement. I could not have been more wrong as I read through the article.

The article gave an account of a young man who, like many Palestinian youth, had written a slogan about liberating Palestine on a wall bordering their village which was near a Jewish settlement and topped with electrically generated barbed wire. Israeli soldiers saw the young man running fast away as they approached. They grabbed him and forced him to erase the slogan he had just written, but not before they turned on the electricity through which his hand would be forced to pass in order to cover the slogan he had just written with paint. The electricity blasted through his hand and aside from the agonizing pain, caused his hand to be literally burnt off. The young Palestinian was petitioning Israel to pay for a prosthetic hand to be made for him in Israel. The woman whose picture I saw at the top of the article was an Israeli official who was trying to block the request. The Israeli government was forcing the man to reapply for a "new hand" over and over, each time telling him, "to try again". I read this article twice and then put the magazine down. I could not believe the violence and the cruelty on the part of the Israeli government. I simply could not register the calculated cruelty toward a young man who really had done nothing violent or actually criminal against Israel. After a while, I went back, incredulous, to read the article again. I could not find it. I looked in the magazine several times and could no longer see where it was. I began to realize that I had "hysterical blindness" and that it was impossible for me to look at that article and photograph of what appeared to be such a lovely person. And so I am now sure that my mind just blotted out the article when I passed that page in the Time magazine.

CHAPTER 27

On my return from Israel in 2001, I read in the weekend edition of the Herald Tribune, August 21-23 of how three Palestinian men were crossing into Israel for their daily jobs as delivery men in a supermarket in Tel Aviv. As they passed through the checkpoint, they were detained and taken outside into the rain where they were beaten and, (all three were of slight build), then thrown up against a wall breaking bones in each of the men's bodies. They were then forced to drink their own blood which the Israeli soldiers scooped off the wall. The soldiers then took their pictures and shoving them into the faces of the barely, semi-conscious terrorized men, told them that if they ever saw them again, they would kill them. When the three men reported what had happened to their boss and why they had been absent from work, the owner of the supermarket who was also a rabbi, was furious and went to the press with this story. When the details of the case were presented to B'TSelem, the oldest and first human rights organization in Israel, the spokeswoman commented that B'TSelem received similar reports on a monthly basis and that the only reason this horrifying and unbelievable incident got into the press was because the men's' boss, the rabbi, was someone who was outraged enough to do something about this brutal attack and went to the media. Eventually the incident was publicized worldwide.

As I traveled in Israel and the West Bank, and read just about everything I could on the region on my return to Mallorca, I could not, simply could not believe that Jews or any group of Jews could be capable of the calculated cruelty documented by many rights groups, against the Palestinian population by Israel.

On another occasion I received information from the Urgent Action Network sponsored by Amnesty International, a program which provides information for participants in the organization to write letters to heads of governments protesting documented human rights violations. In this particular weekly report AI published allegations of child sexual abuse among Palestinian children who were, under the second Infadada, picked up in IDF police vans and transported to jail where children as young as ten were interrogated by Israeli police. These youngsters, accused of throwing stones at Israeli police or other similar misdemeanors could be held without communication with their parents or community for indiscriminate amounts of time before being released. And the report indicated during their detentions many had been subjected to sexual abuse by some members of the IDF.

There is an amazing amount of secrecy on the part of the government in Israel. Even though Israeli publishes one of the best newspapers in the world, Haaretz, which gives open accounts of life inside both Israel and the West Bank, I remember speaking to one Israeli on the subject of Palestinian violations and he replied that he thought the Israeli government was doing everything possible to work for Palestinian rights. And he was quite sincere. Unfortunately, many Israelis refuse to read Haaretz, believing it to be "too left".

There are people in Israel, who, when hearing of disturbing acts of violence against Palestinians will begin to weep. I had such an experience in Neve Shalom-Wahat al-Salaam, the only meshav or community in Israel where Arabs and Jews live together, when I told one lady about the violent abductions of Arab youth in villages nearby by the IDF. The community, founded by Padre Bruno Hussar, a Catholic priest originally from Alexandria, Egypt and himself from a Jewish family, NSWAS sponsors numerous groups from the West Bank who visit the community. I was present for a festival of Bedouins from a village in the West Bank and who showed their authentic artifacts. Often NSWAS arranges visits to Arab villages by international travelers who visit there. I was invited and went with a group of visitors to meet with Teddy Kollack, the former mayor of Jerusalem, still mayor at the time of my visit, and one of the original participants in the founding of Israel. Mayor Kollock received us warmly and we visited together in his office for a short time. He was very genuine and I felt fortunate to meet with someone of such history and background. I wanted to speak with him longer on how he thought the conflict should be resolved but our time was brief and ended all too quickly.

I have often wondered how Jewish people would be any less connected to the land of Israel and united in their own minds, with their roots there, if the Israelis were to decide to share completely and in a full political sense the land of historic Palestine. Why does Israel not engage in sharing the Holy Land, all of it equally, with the indigenous population of Palestine?

Or how would Israelis be in any way deprived of full lives as Jews through a process of complete sharing? If anything, Israeli lives would be freed from fear of Palestinians who try to get their land back, if a clear political decision was made to liberate the Israeli government from its separatist position.

It does appear, at times, that Israel would rather blow the whole world up instead of concede to democratic norms. Years ago in the 1970's, at Stoneybrook, which is part of the City University of New York and located on Long Island, a conference was held to discuss the crisis in Palestine. The ultimate consensus was that a country whose ultimate criteria for citizenship was a specific ethnicity, that country would inevitably decline into a racist state. Many people left the convention very angry and unaccepting of the verdict. These people continued to believe that Israel was, in fact, justified in claiming the ancient land for an exclusively Jewish state because of the holocaust. In the eyes of others, these people simply refused to acknowledge that two wrongs will never make a right. That the state of Israel cannot deprive the Palestinians of rights to live fully in their own country because of the holocaust which they were not responsible for, in any event.

Noam Chomsky, in his seminal work "The United States, Israel and the Palestinians", has a last chapter entitled, "the Final Solution". The last words of this chapter in this book are a distinct reference not only to the Third Reich, but also to a nightmarish nuclear hell from which "very few will survive" if the Palestinian crisis is not resolved. Is it really possible that the state of Israel and the people governing it are so hardened and isolated in their thinking that they would place the whole world in jeopardy rather than concede to the full institution of democracy in their region?

I myself, after visiting in the region numerous times, really began to feel the inevitability of a worldwide military confrontation, which would originate from the unresolvable Arab- Israeli conflict. It is difficult to describe how amazed I was when I read in the last pages of Noam Chomsky's book, the same conclusion.

Historians of various backgrounds all point to the fact that until the time of the British Mandate, Jews and Arabs, both Christian and Muslim lived together peacefully in the Holy Land. All were Arab-speaking and all shared the same historical, cultural and psychological background. The last sixty year conflict between the Zionists and the people of Palestine, constitutes in the eyes of many observers and historians, particularly Arab academics of the region, a true aberrancy in their relations.

The fact is, that the conflict between Arabs and Jews only arose because a group of Jews from the west, Europe, Russia and North America, espoused the cause of a Jewish homeland in Palestine.

Prior to this time and these political events, Jews and Arabs of Palestine had lived together in harmony. These ethnic groups shared Middle Eastern history, as was just pointed out, culture and relatively close identity. Only with the advent of a group of Jews from the west coming to live in the Holy Land was a conflict created among the Arabs and Jews of the newly divided region.

I never read an Arab writer or journalist, or spoke to any Palestinian on my visits to the region who said Jews from the West had no right to come to live in Palestine. What many Arabs did object to was that the Zionists came into their land and made a war against them, tacitly making the statement that the Arabs had no right to live in the area the Zionists designated for themselves as their nation. And then, once the Zionist statehood was established, the Israelis proceeded to marginalize and to control in every conceivable way, any remaining Arabs still attempting to live in the region. Basically, the position of the Palestinians I spoke to was that they objected to a group of Jews from the west who came and willfully and maliciously deprived them of their land, property, possessions and heritage.

CHAPTER 28

According to the Old Testament, the ancient Israelites were only following the dictate of their God "Yahweh", who commanded them to slaughter all the inhabitants of Canaan because their practices were so evil. The Canaanites worshipped Molech and in one of the worship practices, would heat up a stone idol of their god, Molech, and then place their babies in the statue's arms, immolating them. A German archeologist Otto Eissfeldt, in 1935 claimed evidence around the whole Mediteranean, included ancient Canaan, of exactly this sacrifice. There are various Biblical references to burning and inferences of human sacrifice involving children. Lev. 18:21; 20:2-5; 2 Kings. 23:10; Jer. 32:35. Thus, apparently, the ancient Israelites felt justified in what would be referred to today as "ethnic cleansing".

But the Palestinian people have no such practices, being either devout Muslims or Christians. The two accounts given of the war in 1948 are first, from the Jews. They say that the Grand Mufti of Jerusalem and other Arab leaders told the Palestinians to leave their homes so that the invading Zionists could be removed, by armies from Arab countries, from the land they wanted to create as exclusively for the Jews. After which, the Arab leaders promised, the people of Palestine would be able to return to their homes. And, in fact, many Palestinians did take the keys of their homes with them, just as the Jews had when expelled by the Catholic Kings from Spain. But the Arab armies lost to Israeli forces for reasons often difficult to explain.

There also exists a huge discrepancy between the figures of displaced persons in the 1948 war. Israeli cites a figure of 700,000 non-Jews who were displaced in the war of 1948. But, as has been pointed out earlier, even in Golda Meir's autobiography, she writes of a much higher figure, that altogether, over a million non-Jews of Palestine were forced into exile, forced to flee from Palestine.

The second historical account, is that the Israelis with weaponry created from the metal parts of a dairy farm that went out of business in the U>S. and also arms purchases from Czechoslovakia, ordered people all over Palestine to leave their homes with only what they could carry. This the Zionist army, the Haganah, did at gunpoint. Both these accounts are true. Over one million Palestinians (this is a figure of much dispute in the annals of Israeli history and world history), as has just been stated, Israelis give the figure of 700,000 Palestinians who were displaced in the 1948 War of Independence, and who fled into eastern Palestine and what was to become known as the West Bank which had been previously eastern Palestine. Many hundreds of thousands fled into the Gaza where bewildered Gazans had no idea what was happening or why their area was being flooded with people from Palestine.

Some understood and accepted the aggressive, military actions of the Jews in 1948, (although the extent of Israel's militarism was not clearly understood in 1948 in the West). The whole world had abandoned them to the holocaust when their lives could have been spared and protected by the United States, as well as other countries. At the time that Hitler came to power in Germany, almost every German businessman had a Jewish friend, if you believe the Odessa Files. Germany had produced in the 1930's, the German expressionist art movement, great writers and some of the greatest music of Europe. Suddenly, Germany was rife with filthy tracts spewing racial hatred toward the Jews. The pendulum of high culture and consciousness suddenly swung out of control, and once again, as had been the case historically over centuries in Europe, the Jews became the target of blame and weren't only in danger of decimation, actually many were decimated. Hitler was a member of the Thule society as were many high ranking nazi officers. The Thule society was formed from a secret society, "Order of Teutons". The society itself was started in 1911 by a German World War I veteran, Walter Nauhaus. In fact, all the political power and ideology of the Nazis was a thin cover for what was actually a deeply sinister and potent occult movement, resplendent with the horror of racial inequality and animosity, a passion and sick love for raw power and sadistic feeling for anything or anyone who did not fit the "aryan" model of racial perfection, or who was weak, sensitive or in any way vulnerable.

This experience destroyed the conscience of so many Jewish people, at least among the members of world Jewry that either wittingly or unwittingly supported the barbarity of what was to become the Jewish state. The majority of Jewish people stood by the idea that they could empty out Palestine for themselves in 1948 to create their state. Palestine, now Israel, has been soaked in blood ever since.

I watched a program some years back on TV which interviewed a young man in orthodox dress and skull cap, or yamaka. With great sadness he said he could not understand why only the Jewish people could not have their own state without so many problems. He was very genuine. I longed to speak to him and tell him that he could. But that given the history of the past two thousand years it was now necessary to share it with all the people of Palestine. Why is it an impossible task to explain to modern Israelis the concept of political power sharing with the Arabs of historic Palestine?

And thus is the crux of the Middle East crisis. It is time for the Israelis to accept that the idea of a separatist Jewish state is an outdated idea. If, for example, a journalist tried to depict the average Frenchman, he can no longer write about a man in a jauntily tilted beret, sipping wine in the countryside. The depiction of modern France can just as easily be portrayed as an Arab business man in any large French city or young university student from Africa studying computer science in order to live and work in France.

The Israelis often think of Palestinians and Arabs as dumb and unable to create a modern state in Palestine or share in its administration equally if Israel and the occupied territories were united.

CHAPTER 29

Sitting in the house of an Israeli friend, I was surprised to hear him refer to a badly repaired piece of furniture, as "an Arab job", even though an Israeli had done the bad repair work. This crude and ignorant view of Arabs in general, has, understandably, an immediately, psychologically crippling effect on Palestinians, especially the young, so sensitive and vulnerable, and growing up under Israeli subjugation. Who, because of the many wars in the region have had their educations constantly interrupted and have been frequently subjected to interrogations by the IDF, often the only reason being that they are Arab and therefore suspect of plotting against Israel. I remember looking into the gloomy faces of perhaps seventeen and eighteen year old guys selling me film for my camera near Damascus Gate in the Old City of East Jerusalem, as I reflected on the attitude of Israel toward the Arabs.

I recalled my friend Polly who worked at St. George's Church telling me, as we sat having lunch in a busy cafe in East Jerusalem, that the owner always wanted to be a doctor. But the Israeli government refused to allow him to leave as he wanted to conduct his studies outside the region. "Why", I exclaimed. The Israelis believed that if this man left East Jerusalem and went abroad to be educated, he would most likely tell people in europe or the U.S. about the ongoing crisis, (i.e. the real truth) in Palestine and might even form groups to try to bring the Israeli government down. So the owner of the restaurant where we were sitting had to give up his lifelong dream to be a doctor. As I visited the area and heard stories of the oppressive nature of the Israeli government, I realized that the support, unequivocal support, Israel receives from the West is based on false and manipulated information. To say this support is misguided is an understatement. To say that Israel is the only real democracy in the Middle East is gross hypocrisy and plainly untrue. As has been said many times, Israel is a democracy only for Jews.

CHAPTER 30

I stayed for three weeks in the mid-1990's in Neve Shalom Wahat alSalam, which means "oasis of peace", in Hebrew and in Arabic. NSWAS is the only community in Israel where Arabs and Jews live together. During my stay, I was told a story by one of the international volunteers. In a local kibbutz, after a very long day during the first Intifada, a soldier was loudly recounting some of the "rough" treatment received by Palestinians at his hands and by the other IDF soldiers. The soldier angrily exclaimed "we have to show them (the Palestinians) who is boss". Nearby, in the same room, an older Jewish man looked at the young soldier and said that what he described was very painful for him to hear and that in his eyes the soldiers could not be in the right. The soldier brushed off his remarks by saying "oh, you are just an old man sitting here in the kibbutz all day in safety, you don't know, can't imagine what we soldiers are up against with the Arabs here". By this time the soldier was standing next to the sitting man as they exchanged their words.

Without a word, the old man, staring up at the soldier, lifted his sleeve and the soldier saw that there was the number from the concentration camp the older man had survived and been liberated from by the allied soldiers. The young soldier stared down in shock at what he saw on the old man's arm. Clearly wishing to avoid his gaze as the older man continued to stare up at him unblinkingly, the soldier turned and quickly walked away, all his words of anger against Palestinians suddenly gone.

I was waiting for a bus after traveling in the Negev and staying in a hotel in the local Jewish settlement. As I sat waiting for the bus to visit Encarem, a beautiful spot with a large cave outside Jerusalem, I began to muse about the fact that David Ben Gurion had retired from politics when he was older and went to live in his hut in the Negev desert. There he studied and became a devotee of Zen Buddhism. Without explanation Gurion gave up his belief in "greater Israel", the vast area depicted on the Israeli shekel. It was in this area and completely cut off from his former and truly eventful life as head of Israel that he died.

Two guys sat next to me on the bench in the bus stop and so I struck up a conversation with the one sitting closest to me. He told me they had just finished one of their military assignments. All Israeli men have to go out once a month on military duty. He seemed bone tired. We talked about Jerusalem and he said it was an old, worn-out city and I, although I found Jerusalem fascinating from a historical point of view, agreed with him. We began to talk about all the religious groups living in the Old City and how all orthodox religions and their thinking are outdated and many look upon religions and religious beliefs as relics of the past. I mentioned Tel Aviv and that it was a very alive city which I had very much enjoyed spending time in and had met great people there. He quickly agreed and it turned into an interesting conversation. Since we had just missed the bus and the next one was another hour in coming, we had started to hitch-hike. We saw a car coming toward us and I stood up to make sure we would be seen to be trying to get a lift, waving my arm to try to get the oncoming car to stop. I got up as the car stopped and shepherded the two soldiers toward the car. There was only enough room for two people, so I said to the guy I had been speaking to, "you seem pretty tired so you should get this ride." And I waved goodby as I saw them off. I noticed then, and had before, during my conversation with the one guy, that the other guy was absolutely silent. He was extremely thin and wore, what looked to me, oddly like a pair of plastic girls' sunglasses. So I did not see his eyes and had the distinct impression I would not have liked what I saw in them if I could. Suddenly I became aware of very sinister "vibes" coming from him. The soldier rushed to the far side of the car to get in while his friend went to the other side, and looking up said goodby to me in a pleasant way. I had a very strong feeling his silent partner could not wait to get away from me.

It is a well-documented fact that Hitler was obsessed with the occult. Studying about Hitler's life can give one the impression that this obsession with the dark side of the occult fueled, in fact, the Third Reich, giving it the relentless power its armies marching seemingly endlessly through europe, enjoyed in the first years of the Third Reich. Studying the history of the Third Reich, can, at times, give one an almost uncanny feeling of unnatural forces at work during Hitler's reign. Astrologers have cast Hitler's birth chart and noted that he had a particular configuration in Taurus which indicated cruelty and a strong tendency to sadism. Such attributes were certainly profoundly displayed in the activities of the concentration camps of Europe. I have been shocked at the calculated cruelty of Israel toward the Palestinians and even more shocked at the sickening parallel between those actions and those taken by the Third Reich against Jews. With its huge prisons and army barracks everywhere, Israel gives one the uncanny impression constantly, of the Third Reich. Truly Hitler casts his shadow over Israel.

And the real question on the subject of the Third Reich is, how did a man like Hitler, who was an aspiring artist although he was rejected from the art schools he made application to, subsequently, and with only eight other men initially, create a political party that swept through Europe to the border of Russia and ultimately reduced Europe to ashes? What kind of force of history could conceivably empower such mysterious and largely unexplainable events to take place?

CHAPTER 31

A friend of the community of NSWAS had had his sons abducted from his village by the IDF during the Intifada. I decided to contact this man, Mr. Ankawi. "My sons had to sleep in the trees like birds", Mr. Ankawi told me. IDF soldiers would invade homes in the night and steal young male teenagers so that, according to the Israeli strategy, they would be in prison and could not participate in the rebellion against Israeli occupation. The boys were forced to sign a confession in Hebrew, a language they did not understand. The confession said that they were a threat to Israel and had committed acts of violence against Israeli soldiers. None of this was true. But after a week or so they realized their ill treatment at the hands of their captors which included beatings would not stop. And so they signed the "confession" and were then allowed to eat and sleep in peace. The teenages were also allowed to continue their schooling while in prison as long as they continued "to go along with the soldiers" and not react in any way against their imprisonment. Eventually, after about five years, they were released.

I found out about this man, Mr. Ankawi, from the members of NSWAS. It was Mr. Ankawi who recounted to me these stories of what happened to his sons and other young men of their village. As I entered the village, looking for Mr. Ankawi, I saw two Palestinian girls or young women coming down over the hill next to what turned out to be Mr. Ankawi's house. Their long, beautiful head scarves loosely arranged around their heads blew in the pleasant breeze blowing around us. Their curious looks were directed toward me, as if to say, "who is this girl, does she come from Israel or Europe? Why is she visiting us here today?" They did not speak a word of English but something about their manner was so natural and friendly.

I had been listening to the stories received directly from Mr. Ankawi and a friend and neighbor of his. His friend was actually from a small village very close to Deir Yassin where the previously mentioned atrocities, hidden from the Israeli public for decades, had occurred. The friend of Mr. Ankawi did not stay long. I stood and shook his hand when he left. We had not discussed the massacres. I was afraid it would be too disturbing.

Mr. Ankawi acknowledged that there were some Muslim people and communities in the Middle East that were "too hard". He spoke of being a Muslim and I could see as with many Muslims I had spoken to, how important his faith was to him. He then asked me if I believed in

God. Obviously, since I was not of Middle East descent he did not expect me to be Muslim but it was apparent that he wondered what my religious beliefs would be and I had a feeling it was very important to him that I answer in the affirmative. I told him "yes, I did believe in God." But I did not go into the longer answer I have about the mystery of the universe and my more universal perception of spirituality. That simple question Mr. Ankawi asked me, "do you believe in God" lingers in my mind in a lonely and painful way. Because it is particularly in the "Holy Land" that everyone believes in God and yet unceasing war and gross injustice continues.

I received a lovely lunch from Mr. Ankawi, as we spoke, true to Arab hospitality. When I got up to leave, I had to use the bathroom. Mr. Ankawi's daughters took me to the rear of the house and pointed to a small house or shed, outside, obviously an outdoor toilet. They all made little cries of consternation. They did not want me to see that they only had an outhouse and lacked indoor plumbing. I tried to explain to them that many people in the United States used to have only outhouses before the last war and before the U.S. became so much more affluent than in its earlier days. Unfortunately, they barely spoke English and I don't know how much I was able to communicate to them. But they calmed down and started smiling when they saw it was not a problem for me.

One of the truths that haunts the human race is that the most religious people have often been the most warlike. It seems that man often seeks to create God in his, man's own image instead of the other way around as recounted in Genesis.

Traveling back to NSWAS in a group taxi, I noticed as I got into the car, a lady, all the people who I met were obviously Palestinian. This lady was not dressed in the religious long coat and hijab. She wore modern clothing. She had a dead serious expression on her face as if all the life had been drained out of her. Her expression was so worried and concerned, as if she was in the middle of a war, which she was, and waiting to hear some urgent news. I could imagine that her son or husband had been taken into detention by the Israelis and even been subjected to torture or beating or some horrible treatment banned under the United Nations Declaration of Human Rights.

Also sitting in the group taxi was a Palestinian man. He looked at me with a very serious expression on his face and asked me if I was a journalist.

I replied that I was not but that I was very interested in journalism. I noticed again that both of my fellow passengers wore very serious expressions on their faces and that the atmosphere was grave. It was also obvious that the people here in the West Bank were unaccustomed to seeing non-Palestinians visiting or traveling in their area.

This experience was in such stark contrast to sitting on the beach one Saturday afternoon, Shabbat, in Israel, and watching a large group of Israelis, very comfortably seated in the sand nearby, visiting and sharing lunch. They gave off the feeling of "family". Not only family in the sense of parents and siblings, but of the extended family of a people who were contentedly together in one place, which was for them, the land of Israel. And later as I walked through the streets of Tel Aviv, away from the main boulevards, I could hear the sounds of a large midday meal being shared by families as is the custom, on that Shabbat afternoon. Although very far from their places of birth, North America and Europe, the feeling of "home" wafted out to me through open windows.

What a bitter irony that the happiness of the Israelis I observed that Shabbat afternoon was based on the grinding up of Palestinian lives just short distances away them.

CHAPTER 32

Just before leaving NSWAS, Ahmad, a longtime member of the community warned me, don't say anything about where you were when you go through customs at the airport. "Not even that I was staying here"? I asked, at this community where Arabs and Jews live together. "No" Ahmad replied emphatically. And then he added, "don't say anything about human rights", which the community, (NSWAS) promoted.

When I entered the Gurion airport to take my flight back to Mallorca, I had the worst feeling. It can't just be paranoia because of what Ahmad said, I thought to myself. This feeling is too strong. When asked by the immigration officer where I had stayed during my visit to Israel, I thought, this is really too much, I will just say exactly where I was. So I told the young man that I had stayed in NSWAS, where the community was located, which is outside of Jerusalem near an ancient monastery, called "Latrun". The land, incidentally is still owned by the Vatican on which the monastery stands. The agent looked at me hard. Then he called a woman immigration agent and together we went to a private area. Though I was not subjected to a complete body search, I had to remove most of my clothing and my shoes which were then, with all my other belongings, jacket and purse, searched very carefully. As I came out of this area, the search completed, the original immigration officer looked at my bewildered face in some amusement. I could hear one of his colleagues explaining to him, in the background of the immigration area, all about NSWAS. That the community had been in existence for some time, and was well known to the government. Finally I made my way into the waiting area for my flight out of Israel. But the "bad vibes" I felt were still around me although less in intensity. How did a country purported to be a "Jewish state" based on the great ethics Judaism is founded on ever come to such a situation, where any reference to human rights endeavors and unity among peoples would immediately put Israeli officials on guard and cause suspicion? And if Israel is not founded on Judaism and its ethics, what is it founded on?

CHAPTER 33

Incredibly, an early zionist, Chaim Chassas wrote in 1943, published in Haaretz newspaper, that Zionism was not based on the healing of Judaism but rather on the "uprooting" of Judaism.

The accounts of Israeli atrocities cited here, the man forced to have his hand burned off for only writing a Palestinian slogan, the vicious beatings of men only trying to get to their jobs in Israel because Israel does not allow job infrastructure to develop in the West Bank and the Nazi-like atrocities committed at Deir Yassin are only some of the nightmarish violations made by Israel against Palestine. There are many more injustices and acts of violence against unarmed Palestinians that are not accounted, that are unknown, as the spokeswoman for B'TSelem stated.

The last day I spent in the West Bank before I boarded the minivan which would take me to the airport for my departure from Israel, I spent with some wonderful friends I had met at Beir Zeit University. This university is considered the most prestigious and important center of learning in the West Bank. We had spent the day walking through the village and visited a beautiful church. The two guys I was with were from the university, one from Jericho where he still lived with his family while working on his studies at Beir Zeit, and Tariq, who I had had lunch with and his family in Jericho. The other young man was from a prominent family in Egypt whose family had been living in Palestine but had left when the 1948 war broke out and had recently returned. In the church, the three of us spoke with a young Palestinian lady who was dressed in a sleeveless summer dress, in a relaxed and friendly way. We had all talked about the crisis with a doctor before we left the house where students shared together. The doctor, who practiced in Gaza, had come to visit his family in the West Bank. He said it took nine long, agonizing hours to reach their destination. Normally the drive from Gaza to Jerusalem doesn't take more than four hours. But because all the people on the bus were from Gaza, the travelers were constantly stopped and detained for long periods before being allowed to continue on their way.

Together we had all visited a coffee house where we saw many pamphlets from the Bethlehem Bible College, I had visited in Bethlehem, on the cafe tables. An article in the pamphlet referred to a passage in the Bible describing Christians as "the living stones". Dr. Awad, the director of the college says that we, the believers of the Holy Land who oppose the brutal occupation, "are the living stones the Bible speaks of". My two friends, although Muslim, seemed to relate strongly to the college in the Dheisheh refugee camp and to Mr. Awad, though they were not Christian. They greatly admired the man I had met and spoke with earlier in my trip, in the his office at the Bible College, Bashir Awad. They knew of Mr. Awad's courageous stance against the occupation. Mr. Awad had told me a story of a woman who wanted to contribute to the college but when they got into a discussion about Israel and the woman began to defend Israel by quoting passages from the Bible as many fundamentalist Christians do, about connecting the gathering of the Jewish people back in Israel with the Second Coming of Christ, Mr. Awad explained he could not agree with her having experienced so much opposition to his college from the Israeli government. After futilely disagreeing with each other, he lost the badly needed contribution to the college this lady had intended to make. Even though Dr. Awad explained the constant problems created by the Israeli government for the college, this lady, who supported "Israel" no matter what withdrew her support and funding.

However, Bashir Awad did not fare as badly as the brilliant Dr. Naim Ateek, the founder and director of Shabel, an ecumenical theological center teaching liberation theology in East Jerusalem. After comments published in an Israeli newspaper criticizing the policies of Israel in the West Bank, soldiers had entered his house, broke into his study and confiscated a huge amount of his personal files, some on paper and some on internet. An incredible body of information had been carefully, methodically and studiously compiled, relating to all the work he had conducted in the seminary for a decade. It was all taken or basically, robbed, and unable to reclaim his private property it was possibly even destroyed by the Israelis. There apparently, is no legal power or body in existence in the world today for Dr. Ateek to address himself to, in order to have this writing and his archives, some of it considered by academics and analysts on the conflict in the region to be priceless research on the Middle East events, as well as his religious writings, to be returned to him.

As I stood saying goodbye to my friends and thanking them for the wonderful time I had spent with them, I turned toward the small village of Beir Zeit itself. Suddenly, I was struck with a wave of grief so profound I felt dizzy. The feeling of such sorrow that suddenly and so inexplicably emanated from the village at that moment was in such stark contrast to the wonderful day I had spent with these great Palestinian young people.

I have lived in Manhattan's lower east side in New York, where I witnessed people living in the most derelict conditions, and traveled in India where I saw abject poverty. But I never felt the depth of grief I felt at that moment, as I took my leave from the region, which emanated from the village of Beir Zeit.

CHAPTER 34

The last place I was staying in was the hostel of a large Methodist Church perched on the border of East Jerusalem and West Jerusalem. You could see, on the horizon, the Old City, ageless, as though "pinned" against the skyline in the distance. There was a shop in the Church complex managed by a lady from Costa Rica who had married a Palestinian man. Their shop sold artifacts from Costa Rica. Directly across the street were fine restaurants and a large complex with many modern shops, complete with a movie theater. All this was set in the middle of a park.

In this hostel, I spoke with a worker in the Church from Scotland and a family from the states, the father was Jewish and very much pro-Israeli. In the course of the conversation I interjected, saying that "there is too much pain here". Actually I turned to Barbara, quoting her, what she had said to me in a previous conversation. She looked away and when I repeated what she had said, she simply would not acknowledge the words referring to pain that I had just spoken, actually quoting from our prior conversation. It was as if every conversation had to be censored in the company of anyone proIsraeli. There seemed to be no opportunity to openly express views that would not be welcome to anyone Jewish or in support of the Israeli state. The fact is when I spoke to this man who was from the states and totally pro-Israeli and told him about the ten thousand homes of Arabs in East Jerusalem, scheduled by the Israeli government to be demolished the following year, he looked at me in surprise and concern. He indicated to me as we continued our conversation that he thought such destruction was pretty serious and certainly could not be right. He seemed very surprised and said he thought there must be some mistake in my information. Unfortunately, I was not mistaken. The following year those demolitions occurred.

When I told two friends from England while living in Turkey, some of my experiences while traveling in the region, explaining how Israel expelled so many people in order to make their state, (a fact which many westerners appear to be oblivious of) one exclaimed, "but two wrongs don't make a right". Judging from our conversation this lady had not impressed me as being particularly politically well-informed. While all the political analysts in the world continue to be stumped by the Middle East crisis and how to resolve it, it was truly amazing to hear this lady so succinctly sum up the situation.

Once again I considered the creation of the Balfour Paper, introduced and passed in the British Parliament in 1917. This document gave, virtually vindicated the Jews of the west to establish a Jewish state, enabling them with a "legal" right to invade and occupy Palestine, even against the expressed wishes of the Arab population who all opposed the partition of Palestine and the subsequent creation of a "supremacist" Jewish state.

Although the founders of zionism were not religious, they advocated an extreme form of nationalism, based on the Biblical writing in the Old Testament which states that God ordained that the land of Israel specifically belongs to the Jewish people. Ironically, the ideology of Jewish nationalism or zionism inside Israel today is promoted most heavily among the most religious, and often less educated Israelis.

There was absolute devotion on the part of many Jews who, every Sader, drank the traditional Passover wine after toasting, "next year in Jerusalem". Since their concentrated desires expressed in countless Seder celebrations finally came to fruition, I have reflected how unfortunate it was they did not toast "peace in Jerusalem" as well.

Some years back I read an article about former President Truman who, after the state of Israel came into being, and in its first years when the region was filled with so much violence, was heard to express the view that he had been manipulated into signing accords for the Jewish state and said he had had his "arm twisted" by Chaim Weizmann, then an old man, bedridden in the Astor Hotel in Manhattan, New York. Truman expressed the view that he had never believed it wise for the Jews and western countries to devise a plan to divide Palestine since "all the Arabs were opposed to this plan". And now the region was filled with unceasing hostilities.

The fact is the state of Israel could not be stopped because of American and European inaction during the holocaust. Riddled with guilt and confusion because of the inaction of the west to prevent the holocaust from taking place, and persuaded by the total determintion of the architects of zionism, finally, Truman and others western leaders allowed the state of Israel to come into being. Even though the comments of Truman reveal a great foreboding at the prospect of the division of Palestine and great anger at the subsequent war(s) which transpired between the Arab world and Israel, as a result. the unassailable commitment, coupled with the tragedy of the holocaust, created an inevitable victory for Zionism. Chaim Weissman himself was quoted as saying that the Jewish people have a "pathological" attachment to the Holy Land.

To his credit, Wisemann had always supported nonviolent methods to secure the Jewish state while Ben Gurion had not. Gurion had very quickly assumed a war-like stance as a final resolution to achieving the Jewish state. For his far more respectful approach to the wishes of the Arab world, Wisemann was excluded and often isolated by Ben Gurion and his political allies, such as Golda Meir and others in their growing political efforts to achieve a state. The fact is, in May, 1948 on the very day Gurion, Meir and others signed the Israeli declaration of independence, one principle person who had worked so hard for the Jewish state was conspicuously absent. That person was Chaim Weizmann, who had been assigned to a diplomatic mission forcing him to be away from Israel and thus unable to be present at the momentous occasion of Israel s open declaration to the world that Israel was now a sovereign state.

Jews, and many other people who supported the Jewish state, and who grieved over the horrors of the holocaust with so many lives cruelly and senselessly destroyed, asked the question, "Why cannot Palestine give up such a small amount of territory to the Jews after the Jews have suffered such tragedy"? The view was often put forward and by none other than Golda Meir herself who promoted the idea, that since Jews had done so much to help each other, why couldn't the Palestinians (forced to give up their homes and lives in Palestine) go live in other parts of the Arab world since the Arab world was so large? In fact, all the Palestinians dumped into the West Bank in 1948 by Israeli soldiers were governed at that time by an administration from Jordan.

As discussed previously, Meir made the now notorious statement "there are no Palestinian people". Some historians concede that she was half right. That the Arab population of Palestine was considered part of the greater region of Arab countries. So Golda Meir was not wrong, but given the conflict that transpired, not exactly completely right either. She chose to take a point of view that obscured the real situation and the inevitable ethical problem Israel would have to confront. The situation was that the new Jewish state was based on deception, manipulation and bloodshed. That is, if Palestine had been mostly empty land, if that had been true, as Zionists had claimed, Jews could simply have arrived and safely taken up occupancy in Palestine. Being hardly the case, also obscured was the fact that Palestine had commerce and trade and functioned autonomously. It did have its own economy. Joppa, for example, was a bustling port busy with active trade in the early 1900's. The fact is, Joppa, in particular had been an active and busy trading port for many centuries, since eras long past of the ancient world and continuing on while Palestine was part of four major empires over the past two thousand years.

Many Arabs did agree to some kind of Jewish state and tried to find a solution that would accommodate both communities. But after many discussions all participants were forced to see that for the Jewish state to be formed in any part of Palestine would mean the expulsion of Palestinians, their loss of property and homes, and that this expulsion would be massive. And to imagine it would involve only a few people and families as was originally presented to the international community was grossly inaccurate. Such an expulsion involved well over a million people. This massive expulsion was why the Arab world and Palestinian families have never been able to accept the partition of Palestine and the Jewish state.

Thus, to say that there was "a land without a people for a people without a land" was a terrible lie.

There was a frequent element of racism expressed among early settlers in Palestine, even before Israel became a state. The Jews colonizing the land from the west believed that they had a superior right to Palestine and that their greater expertise as people from the west, qualified them and made them far more eligible, in their eyes, to oversee and control Palestine when the British Mandate expired.

CHAPTER 35

I read in Golda Meir's biography how angry she was when she presented, in the early 1930's her proposal for a Jewish state to be created in Palestine, to the World Socialist Organization. At that time, the World Socialist Organization was comprised almost entirely of Jewish people. But to Meir's great surprise and unhappiness, to a person, the members of the WSO, all decried the idea of returning to the ancient land of Palestine and "carving out" a state there. The people in the WSO said that such an action was counterproductive to ending the scourge of anti-Semitism and that the adoption of worldwide socialism would be the answer to the problem of anti-Semitism. The people of the organization said, further, that carving a state for Jews in Palestine would very likely cause much conflict in the region and even might lead to war. The past sixty years have shown how right they were.

The issue of secrecy comes to the fore in any serious examination of Israel in the past sixty years. Just prior to the Israeli invasion of Lebanon in the 1970's, an American Naval ship was stationed in the harbour near Haifa. Israeli forces bombed this ship, the U.S.S. Liberty, the result being that around thirty American Navy Men were injured and three Navy officers lost their lives, during this bombardment. It is supposed by political analysts that Israel suspected the American Navy ship of surveillance activities. The Israelis were very concerned that the U.S. would learn of their intentions to invade Lebanon and try to dissuade them or prevent them from doing so. Thus Israel was determined that the Americans not know that Israeli military were just ready to invade Lebanon. The subsequent invasion of Lebanon under the leadership of former Ariel Sharon resulted in the massacres of the people in the Palestinian refugee camps of Shatila and Sabra. These atrocities received worldwide condemnation and also much protest inside Israel.

The American families who actually lost their loved ones to Israel's bombardment had a long and bitter battle with the U.S. government to have their husbands, fathers and brothers receive the military metals due to be awarded to them posthumously as well as military burials. The U.S. did everything possible to ignore the requests of the families, trying desperately to cover up the incident, that a U.S. navy ship was bombarded by a close ally, Israel, but after a good number of years, gave in to the requests of the families for the remains of their loved ones to be buried with full military honors. Paul Findley, a Republican Senator from Illinois, now deceased, wrote a book detailing the entire incident as well as other American - Israeli cover-ups. The book is entitled "They Dare To Speak Out".

CHAPTER 36

I was on my way out of Bethlehem to Jerusalem on a bus whose passengers were Palestinians. As I entered the bus to take my seat, I brushed my arm lightly against a Palestinian woman who, though it was hot summer, was dressed in an angle length, long sleeved dress of what looked like very heavy material. Our eyes met for a second. She smiled tentatively and then her eyes changed and there was the most imploring look in them. It was almost as though she said to me in a whisper, "help us, please help us", her attempt to communicate was so intense. Then she moved to take her seat, and the moment so real and with her message so clear, was gone.

Suddenly, the bus stopped and a very stockily built and gruff Israeli soldier came on board, demanding to see everyone's documents. Even I was a little afraid. I told the soldier that I was from the United States and that my passport was in the meshav, "community" where I was staying. He said that was fine, although in a very serious tone which made me feel that I had better stay on my toes. He said to me, again very seriously, "I was born in the United States, I remember my country". This surprised me because he had an accent and was obviously an Israeli. Frequently, and in this case, unusually, I was reminded of the unique connection between Israel and the United States.

We all had to disembark the bus and wait for the Israeli security to allow us passage into Jerusalem. The street was filled, mobbed, with Palestinians from Bethlehem struggling to see what the problem was and why they couldn't get the few miles into Jerusalem. I reflected how, for centuries, the people here had passed freely between Bethlehem and Jerusalem. And now their lives were horribly inhibited and oppressed by the tyranny of the Israeli government which can arbitrarily detain them for undetermined amounts of time. I observed, in particular, one Arab man in his fifties, terribly distraught, struggling to explain his errand and how important it was for him to get to Jerusalem, to a very young looking Israeli soldier who looked down at this Arab man, obviously from a family with very long ties to the Holy Land. The soldier, with an air of someone who believes he has absolute control and absolute right to that control, remonstrated in a condescending and patronizing way with this man, many years his senior, as if he was a simple child that he was having difficulty reasoning with.

I wished desperately that I could do something to help the Palestinians get through the congested checkpoint, but realized I was completely helpless in this situation. The gruff soldier who had ordered us all off the bus, came up to me and smiling in a friendly way, found a Palestinian man who took me into his car and that apparently, the soldiers at the checkpoint knew. As we sped off to Jerusalem, the man told me he had visited Los Angeles and how aggressive all the "Jews" were there, during his visit. I really objected to this stereotypical characterization. I had certainly known many Jews, and found them to be really friendly and supportive people. I listened and wanted to object to his stereotype but judging from the authoritarian Israeli action we had both just witnessed, and beleaguered from that unhappy and very stressful situation at the checkpoint we had just escaped, I slumped down in my seat and could not reply.

CHAPTER 37

I watched a program on Press TV which showed an amazing conference taking place somewhere in the West Bank, of Israelis and Palestinians speaking together, in the most serious and moving way about how they believed the Middle East could change and become a "place of love" for everyone. It was very spiritual and the people, as they communicated their message, conveyed an almost metaphysical feeling to the audience and to the many people standing on a platform above a larger group. When the program ended, I felt as though I had been transported to a realm quite outside the human one, if only for just a very brief time. Hearing these people speak together of a vision of the Middle East without war was quite unlike anything I had ever encountered in my travels to Palestine and studies of the Middle East. There was a feeling in this broadcast, as the people in it were shown and heard speaking together about making peace in the region that was markedly and strangely mysterious, and wonderful.

I heard on the World Service, the BBC radio news, a rabbi from North Africa speak about the era of the Messiah. When the Messiah comes he said, according to the Jewish tradition, there will be no more war. Everyone will have food to eat. There will be peace and justice, without exception, all over the world. As the rabbi spoke on this radio program, I could feel how deeply he believed what he was saying to be true. And as I listened, I could feel a "lightness" emanating from and surrounding his words, almost moving out of the radio and enveloping me in the rabbi s amazing belief in such a wonderful future for the human race. I understood the rabbi speaking to mean that the reign of the Jewish Messiah does not involve only Jewish people but this reign extends to the whole planet and everyone on it.

My thoughts returned to Dr. Awad as I spoke to him with other Palestinians who brought me there. I told him I hoped to write about my experiences while traveling in the West Bank. At the end of our conversation, Dr. Awad said in a tired and resigned way, "I hope you can tell others about the real situation here, our despair when the rest of the world turns their backs to us, while so many hardships are placed continually on our people. We need all the help we can get." I am still carrying his words with me and still working, I hope, by writing, to shed the much needed light on the Middle East crisis, achieve the end of Israeli dominance and injustice and bring justice and security to the Palestinians. As a statement of faith, I write here, that I will continue to try to find ways to work toward this end for the rest of the life, as are many other Jews, non-Jews, activists inside Israel and human rights supporters throughout the world.

CHAPTER 38

I cannot stress enough my reflection of how Hitler, with his obsession of the sinister side of the occult released a horror of evil, "demons", into the human sphere. Whether a person believes this figuratively or literally, does not matter. The unfortunate and horrifying results are the same. The Third Reich collapsed the Jewish psyche, turning all the great contributions of Jews for centuries to dust. When one sees the carnage wrought by Israel in the West Bank and Gaza either in person or in the media, such reports unequivocally show how the inception of the state of Israel in 1948 destroyed Jewish culture, ethics and the very soul of the Jewish people. When I saw the faces of some Israelis both travelling and on televised news reports, they looked so hard and strange to me, I am reminded of some of the German people who knew about the atrocities against the Jews (and others) during WWII, and did nothing.

I keep seeing a nuclear holocaust engulfing our planet if Israel does not undergo a transformation and create a completely democratic society in the territories it now occupies.

When I look online I now see many human rights organizations, often comprised of young people who are adamantly denouncing their country, inside Israel. And very publicly doing so. The organizations are demanding democracy for all in the region, just as activists in South Africa did before ending its apartheid regime. And end its state supremacy the government of Israel, will. Just as at the height of Nazi power in Europe, the seeds of failure were already apparent to many inside the SS, the Third Reich, did in fact fall. For many reasons the Third Reich could not support its war effort. But in a larger sense, its evil could only exist as long as human beings have failed to take responsibility. The same is true in Israel, with so much information now widely distributed in the west exposing the reality of Israeli cruelty and the dire extent of its injustice, enough people in the international community, will, inevitably, force Israel to unite the territories, or some would same reunite, and institute democracy.

Exhausted, walking from Jaffa toward my hotel on Hayarkon Street which borders the Mediterranean Sea in Tel Aviv, I hailed a taxi and began a conversation starting with me complaining about my feet, with the taxi driver, a serious, plain-speaking man of middle age. This man told me he had grown up in Joppa with the Arabs, who he called "great people". He said he wished the Palestinians had the whole west bank for their state and Jerusalem as their capital shared with Israel. He spoke of the war in Lebanon with sorrow, he had lost two sons in the Israeli invasion of that country which military action, my driver said he had not supported. When we passed the Labor Party headquarters as we rode toward my hotel, he slowed and glared at the office. He spoke disparagingly of their policies, with words to the effect, "what are they up to now". It was clear this man did not support any Israeli political party at all and viewed the entire Israeli political apparatus with much suspicion. His views were so far from the attitude of the two girls who had taken my fee to enter the museum of Ilana Goor, a well-known Israeli artist, in Joppa. When I mentioned something about the Palestinians living in Jerusalem in the course of a conversation on the region, they suddenly both went icily silent.

I took a west bank "jitney", which is a group taxi, to the village of Qalqilya. I was so interested to see first-hand what the small Arab village was like. The taxi took me into an isolated region where I could no longer see cars in any direction on the small country road. The driver stopped and pointed to an empty road which turned right and inclined slightly upward in the distance toward my destination, according to the driver. He told me to walk on that road, it was not too far, he said, and I would reach Qalqilya. I saw as the taxi sped away in another direction that it was 3:00 in the afternoon and I realized it certainly should not be any later than that hour in this remote area to have arrived at my destination. I had, after all, to return to my hostel at the Methodist Church in Jerusalem, before dark.

After walking about fifteen minutes, I did, in fact, soon see a few houses on either side of the road. As I glanced up to the right I saw a restaurant filled with people eating a late lunch. And coming slowly toward me was an older Arab man, keffiyeh on his head, stepping down the stairs of the eating place, who reached out a welcoming hand to me. As he kindly led me into the restaurant which I surmised must be owned by him, I realized I was hungry. I had not eaten since breakfast. People sat together at long tables and as I ordered the delicious food of the region, salad, falafel and humus, the later made from garbanzo beans, I struck up a conversation with two men from Israel sitting next to me. I saw that the whole table and restaurant was filled with Israelis who, the men I sat speaking with, informed me were a group that they were part of. They had come in a bus and were touring the region that day, visiting a Roman site, and now having lunch. As we spoke, I told these men I thought the region should be completely united. One man said, "But what would happen to the Jewish state then", in a very serious and urgent tone. I said I thought it would really finally emerge once all the regions were united. The man did not understand my reasoning. But the other was very kind and showed, in contrast to the defensiveness of many Israelis on the subject of the conflict, great forbearance. He even expressed some openness to my idea. When I finished lunch, and was saying goodbye to the two, thanking them for the conversation we had, the second man I spoke to insisted on paying for my lunch. Thanking this man for his generosity, I told him and his friend again, how much I had enjoyed our conversation. As we exchanged our last words, I was impressed with their genuine kindness to me.

As I looked at the roman ruin nearby, I realized how similar in this respect all of the Mediterranean is from end to end, with its countless Roman ruins, reminding the traveler of the vast extent of the Roman Empire. I then saw the Israelis, in the distance, all boarding their bus to head back to Israel. I walked up the road further and saw a picnic area, shop and small tourist area filled with travelers. I asked some people if there was more to see in the town nearby, and they told me there was an older area, and gestured for me to go down a path that I could see nearby. I turned the corner and came up to a very old building that some villagers gathering around me, told me was a Christian Church. I could see signs of people being in it, cushions were scattered around on the floor in front of an altar. It was obviously still in use though appeared to be quite old. It was getting late and I knew I would have to return and organize my journey back to Jerusalem. As I started up the path to the area where the tourists were gathered, an excited villager came up to me and pointed a good distance down the street where he said another Christian Church was. I wondered what it looked like inside, then another man came up to me and very insistently said, you must come with me back to the cafe or you will be lost. As the afternoon sun was considerably lower, I quickly agreed. When I arrived back I asked how much a taxi cost and luckily was able to get a ride back with a group in a taxi who had come from Jerusalem and had room for one more person. We passed Nablus on our return, whose long souk stretches the length of the city and I remembered walking through its ancient streets and what a wonderful experience it had been seeing those crumbling walls lined with so many fascinating artifacts. But in the end, it was getting dark by the time we started back to Jerusalem and the driver bruskly informed us it was too late to go walking in the souk. He seemed very anxious to return to the city. Upon our arrival I thanked the people who had let me ride with them and everyone quickly went their own way as it was now completely dark. I was fortunately, near the hostel, and had to rush quickly away from the taxi driver who, though the group who took me insisted the fare had all been paid both ways in advance, wanted me to pay more. I felt unsure about paying him more, he was so demanding and unfriendly. I was so grateful for the wonderful day I had spent, the kindness of the Arab owner of the restaurant who beckoned me into the busy cafe where I had lunch, and the generosity of the two Israelis who I had visited with, in paying for it. I was lucky to have met at the very end of the day, when it was getting dark, people who were returning to Jerusalem. There is very little, if any, tourist infrastructure in the West Bank.

CHAPTER 39

I read in a Palestinian publication how many wells that spring from underwater aquifiers which have existed for centuries in the West Bank are being desiccated by Israelis in adjacent townships who find ways to siphon off water from the wells to use in their plentiful swimming pools and other daily water needs. This leaves the Palestinians in the villages with "not a drop of water to drink", one Palestinian woman in a village near a huge settlement, was quoted as saying. The people interviewed in the article published in the "Palestinian Chronicle" spoke of the "agony", that was the word used, imposed on them constantly, as a result of the Israeli occupation.

I saw on a Press TV report, how in Hebron the Palestinians have to barricade themselves into their homes. Their formerly outdoor areas, porches, have to be covered completely with wire that fences them in on every side. The journalist said these Palestinian people report dead animals being thrown on top of the wiring and even feces can land on these wire defenses covering Palestinian homes. I watched an Israeli woman go right up to the fence where Arab women in hijab and long-sleeved, full length dresses sat quietly together, and then as someone brought in tea, the Israeli woman hissed in the most horrible and crazy way, "whores, whores". The women began to scream and leaping up from their chairs, ran, racing into their house away from this woman hissing the most unbelievable insults at them like some kind of evil snake.

While visiting in the West Bank, also near Hebron, a settlement town, I began a conversation with an Israeli man in military uniform while waiting for a bus to go back to Jerusalem. I had tried to get off the bus at the local market in Hebron but had been stopped by soldiers, also travelling on the bus who told me that it was "too dangerous, any time a bomb can go off". So I had gotten off at a settlement town and had lunch in a cafe in front of the bus stop. Wandering around the township I had observed Israelis going about the business of their daily lives, shopping, and several women had small children in tow. The atmosphere, even in this small Israeli township was charged with an excitement that I could only recall experiencing in San Francisco's Haight-Ashbury, many years ago, in 1967. In both areas the air was charged with a singlular exciement. As I began to speak to this tall and heavily built man, he told me honestly that the people in Hebron did everything possible to intimidate and harass the Arab population. He said that he had grown up in Hebron, and as child, relations between the Jews and Arabs were compatible and harmonious.

There was no conflict at that time between the two groups. He told me that he would far rather be at home with his wife and family in Israel than out patrolling in Hebron where he could clearly observe Israeli settlers making life so difficult for the Arab families.

Finally he said, "I guess I am just here protecting myself". I found this statement curious because he lived in Israel and himself, had only had good relationships with Arabs when, in the past, his family had lived in Hebron. Who was he protecting himself from, dressed in full military gear? I had wanted to go and visit Abraham's Tomb before returning to Jerusalem.

The man told me that the ancient site was very close by, just a short walk. However, in no uncertain terms he warned me not to go there. "Big men, fully armed like myself go there and never come back", I was told. Reluctantly, when the bus to Jerusalem stopped, I boarded it. I turned around and waved goodbye to the man I had just been speaking to. He, also smiling, and waved back. As I took my seat, I glanced out, and could see his pleasant and friendly face in the crowd as he too waited for another bus to a military installation. I wondered, deep down inside, what he really thought about the Israeli government and its policies. The conversation was another example of the tremendous confusion surrounding the events taking place in Israel and the West Bank everyday, all the time.

In another West Bank township, an Israeli man raced after a little boy from the nearby arab village. Though the child was only playing, because he was in close proximity to the Jewish township, the Israeli became quite agitated. Running up to the Palestinian boy he grabbed him before the startled child could escape and actually bit off his ear. This was an account from a 1990's issue of Time magazine.

CHAPTER 40

I read a story of a group of Israelis in the 1950's who wanted to go to Germany and indiscriminately bomb German cities in retaliation of the silence of the German people during the holocaust. But David Ben Gurion refused to support such a plan, saying it was far better for Jews to stay in Israel and go on fighting the Arabs to protect the Jewish state. But clearly, the idea of vengeance was in the minds of these Israelis who wanted to terrorize German citizens if they had gained support to do so.

Carl Jung's elucidation of the "shadow", one of the most potent archetypes in the pantheon of archetypes is a unique study of human behavior. The Greek philosopher Aristotle is credited with creating the concept of archetypes. Jung continued the exploration of this concept, which is that of prototypical ideas or forces that recur over and over historically but that cannot be completely explained or analyzed. In his discussion of the "shadow", Jung warned of the repression of ideas or of actions, that when finally expressed can be wholly destructive. The Jews, historically, held themselves to a higher standard and the world was certainly and without a doubt, a better place for it, as Jews historically set great examples of ethics and humanism. But when the Nazi holocaust befell the Jews and not one government in the west stopped their torture and attempted extermination, the result was a monstrous emergence of the shadow. The zionists "dumped" centuries of Jewish ethics in their bloody construction of Israel. When reviewing Israeli human rights violations, the nazi shadow looms large, unspeakable and deathly.

As I traveled down from Safed, a city in the far north of Israel which has been a center of Kabbalistic study and writing for centuries, I noticed a very young and slightly built Israeli girl traveling on her own. When I changed bus in a large town in the center of Israel, to go onto Encarem, the beautiful area outside Jerusalem, where there is a large cave and hostel, she came up to me and asked me where I was going and made sure I had the right bus and good directions. She spoke so quietly and softly and extended herself in such a particularly kind way to me, I seriously contemplated the stories of angels living among us in human form and that she might be one of them.

I had visited Safed so I could attend some classes on the Kabbalah. I found a nice and inexpensive place to stay. In the morning I went along the street directly outside, following the narrow cobblestone path to what appeared to be a very large hotel. As I looked around to see if there was an area where people were eating breakfast, a large and imposing lady walked up to me, her eyes, though early in the day, were heavily made up. In an almost hostile and very commanding way, she asked me, "what do you want"?, I said, I was looking for breakfast and thought this was a hotel where I could eat. She promptly said no, that it was not a hotel, it was a private area. I remembered someone telling me there was a "war" situation in that corner of Israel (though exactly how this small area was somehow a "war area" was not explained) where Safed is. After speaking to this lady, I guessed that was the "situation" I had run into. I had the impression the area was serving as living quarters for the combatants of the "war situation".

That night I attended one of the classes in the Kabbalah center. I asked the rabbi what relationship the Bible had to the Kabbalah. Without hesitation he replied, "The Bible comes from the Kabbalah".

Upon visiting the states, I told my niece this story. A devout Christian, she replied "I don't know about that". I had to remind her that, since the Jews wrote both the Bible and the Kabbalah, I think the Jews should know.

While staying in my hostel in Safed, I met and spoke with an Israeli man whose background was Middle Eastern and, as such, stretched much time back into the history of Iran. Eli, my acquaintance from Iran, took me to meet an older couple who lived on the outskirts of Safad and had lived in Israel since its very beginning, in 1948. It was obvious that Eli was good friends with this couple who greeted us both very warmly. The lady was an accomplished painter and I truly enjoyed looking at her lovely watercolors. They served us tea and I told them about my paintings, which centers around my study of sumi-e, Japanese ink painting. They were all so interested to hear about the study of my artwork with Koho Yamamoto in New York. This lady and her husband were both so kind and special. I will never forget them.

I recall in my conversation with Eli, how his Arab-Israeli and Palestinian employees would tell him many times that it was so great to work for him.

They privately expressed the view that they found many Israelis to be really crass in the way they expressed themselves. The Arab employees told Eli that the modern Israelis occupying their country had no class, no graceful manners and were lacking in all civility. They told Eli they thanked God he was from "their part of the world". Being Jewish had nothing to do with their relationship. The primary factor was his Iranian and Middle Eastern background which, in their eyes, enabled Eli to treat them, as Arab employees, with a quiet and respectful regard.

An example of what the Arab employees of Eli was referring to is as follows.

As I moved through the throng of the many people entering the Church of the Holy Sepulchre inside the Old City, I saw, sitting high up on a group of bleachers on one side of the courtyard, a young Israeli, perhaps only in his early twenties, dressed in full military uniform. Speaking quite loudly into his mobile phone, I could hear his voice, high-strung and unbelievably tense. He exuded danger and trouble. He was a soldier who, fully armed, held life and death in his hands. The very idea of this young man with all his armour and military gear entering a small Palestinian village, was terrifying. The Palestinians have no military or legal body to protect them. They are at the mercy of the Israeli government and its dictates. I think of the Arab family I visited in a refugee camp in Ramallah while on a tour. From what I understood of the study of the region, the people I could see in the camp had become more and more conservative, the women wearing more and more clothing, as if that would somehow protect them, and indeed, such dress is a psychological statement of "protection". Not having access to quality education, their lives are a hopeless huddling together. The Palestinians in this camp and others similar to them, become hardened to the point where some actually carry out suicide bombings. Believing if they give up their lives and kill a few Israelis they are making a statement that their situation is dire and they desperately need protection. But the world, so lacking in information on the Middle East is even more confused and thinks the Palestinians are crazy and Israel is justified somehow in having to militarily control them. In this refugee camp, so close to Jerusalem and other areas with parks and greenery, the streets are literally, concrete.

When the U.N. made these camps they allowed for no green. Just covered every walkway with thick cement.

CHAPTER 41

In 1947, Golda Meir visited the now historically infamous camps of Jewish refugees in Cyprus, who were desperately struggling to get into Palestine and detained by the British from doing so. She was reportedly attacked on one occasion by one of the detained Jews who loudly disclaimed her efforts to free them, i.e., the Jews in these camps, and get them into Palestine and freedom. Her attacker said she was not militant enough in her efforts to liberate them out of these camps in Cyprus. Although their situation was admittedly dire, these same Jewish refugees struggling to get into Palestine are reminiscent of those who carried out the horrors in Deir Yassin. And once again, one is confronted with the terrors practiced by some Jews to empty Palestine of as many of the indigenous Arab population as possible. And once again, glaringly evident is the fact, "that two wrongs will never make a right".

Golda Meir also struggled against Jewish terrorists who frequently attempted to extort money from the Jews of Palestine at that time to continue their violent attacks against the British, often involving blowing up British properties and installations. These efforts against the British were carried out by the Palmach, a Jewish army that existed during the British Mandate.

Ships full of Jews from the camps in Cyprus tried desperately and often unsuccessfully to escape the camps in Cyprus and get into Palestine which they considered to be their only refuge. Sixty percent of the homeless survivors of war-torn Europe were Jews placed in Cyprus camps who had survived the death camps of the Nazis and had been liberated out of them by the Allied forces. They had, at one point, been boxed in cages like animals, and forced by the British to sail to Germany, where British soldiers physically forced the Jews, 400 of whom were pregnant women, to disembark on German soil. This took place in 1947. It is incredible to note that on finding out about the carnage wreaked by the Nazis, and incarceration in death camps of millions of Jews alone, one British official remarked to Golda Meir's face, "that the Jews must have done something to make the Nazis react against them in this way". To read this account of such a conversation taking place between a high-ranking British official and Golda Meir, is like being slapped against the wall. The idea that anyone in power in Britain could make such a statement, is hard to believe. One begins to understand how and why some Jews or Zionists went completely mad and mindlessly wreaked such violence against the Palestinians, but who, after all had nothing to do with the holocaust or British policies. Again and again, it was the

Palestinians who were made to pay the price of the holocaust with their own, the Nakba, which in Arabic means, "disaster".

Many writers, historians and journalists have tried to write about and make sense of the inception of Israel in 1948 and the events leading to it, but it is a confusing, bewildering and finally completely confounding task. Unable to come to any ethical conclusion, many researchers try to take sides but end in a hopeless quandary. It is truly impossible to take completely either side, is the conclusion of many. Israel and the Palestinians have been struggling with a two state solution for sixty years and still not been able to accomplish it. Most dissidents in the region and activists outside it, now consider a full institution of democracy as the ultimate and only solution in the region.

Although the British Parliament had passed the Balfour and White Papers in favor of a Jewish state, and President Truman advocated one hundred thousand Jews be allowed to enter Palestine, all the western nations did not want to vote for and be responsible for a partition of Palestine that the Arab nations would never agree to.

However, that partition did take place even though forty eight percent, not a majority, voted for the partition, while the whole Arab world voted against it in the United Nations. Because of the failure of the proposition to reach fifty percent, the request for partition never even came in to the Security Council for its final vote and acceptance. On May 14, 1948, the Israelis simply opted to declare their own state, the land of Israel, sovereign and free.

CHAPTER 42

Many people make the comment that the conflict between Israelis and Palestinians and referred to by some as the "Middle Eastern puzzle", continues unabated because Israel makes so much money from the production of armaments. That Israel produces and stockpiles a serious amount of arms, including nuclear warheads, is a well-known fact. But exactly how many warheads, missiles capable of massive destruction, Israel actually has stockpiled is not clear. It is believed that Israel has at least four hundred of these missiles of destruction in its vast arsenal, if not more.

I found the Palestinian residents of Neve Shalom - Wahat al Salam (NSWAS) to be very deferential in their comments on the conflict and in the manner in which they spoke. But, one young Arab man said, as we spoke about Ben Gurion, "he was a great man for his people". This was in answer to my question of what did he think about Israel's first leader and prime minister. He left out, "but not for Arabs". But it was implicit in his answer. The first priority of Ben Gurion was definitely not making peace but establishing a Jewish state, "whatever that took". Which, obviously included a lot of bloodletting on Palestinian soil. He and Golda Meir, though saddened by the prospect of war were not in Palestine to achieve peace in that region but a Jewish state, and by whatever means.

Again in Time magazine in the 1990's I read an article about a family in Gaza who established a very successful T-Shirt business. But as their profits rolled in, so did Israeli taxes. Eventually, the draconian amount of taxes Israel demanded from the small but very successful company drove it out of business. Mad with grief and rage, one of the sons' in this family drove through a Gazan checkpoint loaded with bombs and blew himself up along with several other Israeli soldiers. His sister, also driven beyond reason, told the reporters who interviewed her immediately after the incident, "this is the happiest day of our lives". No one can answer the question that beggars the mind. Why, why on earth does Israel employ such brutal and unfair policies, policies that can only and inevitably lead to Israel's own destruction?

So many books have been written about Israel and the Palestinians and their conflict. Why write more on the subject? The answer is that there are so many people who clearly do not understand the massive scale of injustice and cruelty that continues in the region, and that unabated, could lead to an equally massive military conflagration drawing the whole world into it. Not to mention that fact that U.S. taxpayers are footing the bill for Israel's policies, as as been pointed out, Israel is the largest recipient of U.S. foreign aid.

It is horrifying to review these accounts, well documented by journalists and the people of the region themselves. Yet the international community continues to refer to Israel, "as part of the family of nations". Particularly shocking are the evangelical Christians who countenance Israel as an "object" they almost worship, giving it their total credence, and who refuse, on a wholescale level, to make themselves knowledgeable of the massive and calculated cruelty of Israel against the Palestinians.

I was with an Israeli friend driving from Tel Aviv to Jerusalem. Suddenly, he turned off the highway onto a side road paralleling the highway we just turned off of. Turning to me he said, "Watch this". He took the car out of gear, and although we were on a completely straight road, the car started rolling backwards, slowly at first and then it gained some momentum. My friend, Avi Noam, had to stop the car or it would have continued to roll. Avi Noam said, no one can explain this. Later he showed me ruins outside Jerusalem in a valley, perhaps three thousand years old.

I have read that the Jewish people are governed by Saturn. Every person, country, and place has a particular planetary influence. In astrological terms the influence of Saturn is one of the most difficult and harsh to be influenced by. Saturn, which represents the remorseless, ultradisciplined, and authoritarian father, is considered the most draconian astrological influence.

I am not writing to promote astrology in particular. But on reading about the influence of Saturn over the Jews I was struck by another example of the wholly unique history and narrative of Jews. Tried and tested beyond endurance it appears that the zionists gave into the evil power of the Third Reich. In their relentless quest of some for a Jewish state, the zionists allowed themselves to become a continuance of the nazism and virtually become the agents of the very force that threatened to decimate them.

CHAPTER 43

Theodore Herzl, as stated previously, an Austrian newspaper man, living in the late 1880's is considered to be the founding father of modern zionism and the resultant Jewish state in Israel. His vision of zionism or return to Palestine to create a Jewish state came about when he was covering the Alfred Dreyfus trial in Paris in 1894. Dreyfus was a Jew indicted for treason in France. Eventually, these allegations proved to be false and he was exonerated. However, as Herzl stood on the Champ -Elysees in the middle of Paris covering the trial, he was horrified to see a large crowd forming who were shouting "kill the Jew, kill the Jew". Herzl returned to Vienna a broken man, convinced that the scourge of anti-Semitism so infected the Gentile world that Jews would never be safe from antiSemitism. Because of this it was imperative that the Jews achieve their own state. Herzl came to believe, largely because of his coverage of the Dreyfus trial, (although this was later denied, some historians cited other reasons as well) that Jews had no hope or chance of survival without their own state.

Thus, one reads about Herzl willing to employ the most bizarre and deviant means to achieve the objective of a Jewish state. He even said he would support disinvestment and try to bankrupt Jewish businesses, that is, make life very difficult for Jews in the west, in order to get support for that state.

A letter was found in the Foreign Ministry of Israel written in 1958, by Golda Meir, sent to Israel's ambassador to Poland, to Katriel Katz, and marked "top secret". In this letter Golda Meir stipulated, "Don't send me sick or disabled Jews". She also wrote that she hoped this request to Katz would not "harm immigration". Admittedly it was rough going in Palestine. When Golda Meir first arrived in 1921, she describes what is now the area of Tel Aviv as a bug-ridden swampland. But still, the reader is compelled to ask the troubling question was not the zionist state formed to help and assist in every way all Jews? One imagines the Jews liberated out of the nazi death camps. Some, if not most, were barely alive. These writings now beg the sad question, was Golda Meir just a ruthless politician?

Aside from this question, and to Meir's credit, it remains a fact that she worked very hard for the state of Israel to create developmental programs in Africa that were very successful and much admired by other countries.

Both Sigmund Freud and Albert Einstein were supportive of some of the efforts of Jewish settlers in Palestine and both members of the Board of the prestigious Hebrew University, although both men remained very wary and critical of the full implementation of zionist policies. Neither man ever supported a Jewish state that would rob the Palestinians of their homes and property. Both men were proud of the Hebrew University but both clearly rejected the idea of a militarized Jewish state.

On April 17, 1938, Albert Einstein, in a speech he gave at the Commodore Hotel in New York City, to the National Labor Committee for Palestine, said, "I should rather see reasonable agreement with Arabs on the basis of living together in peace than the creation of a Jewish state".

He continued ….. "Apart from practical consideration, my awareness of the essential nature of Judaism resists the idea of a Jewish state with borders, and army, and a measure of temporal power no matter how modest. I am afraid of the inner damage Judaism will sustain especially from the development of a narrow nationalism within our own ranks against which we have already had to fight strongly, even without a Jewish state." Accounts quote Einstein as saying, "It would be my greatest sadness to see Zionists do to Palestinian Arabs much of what Nazis did to Jews." Later historians claim this statement was falsely attributed to him. Einstein never supported a Jewish state, and only the partition of Palestine if Arabs agreed to it. However, when he died, a Jerusalem newspaper falsely and without shame claimed Einstein had supported a Jewish state. Einstein had always said he only supported "a safe haven" and not a Jewish state. Given the falsely reported view (of his support for a Jewish state) of Einstein after his death, it is quite possible to imagine that he did, in fact, make a statement to the effect he hoped zionists would not repeat to Arabs what nazis did to Jews.

Lord Montagu, a member of the British Parliament and himself a Jew, criticized the early zionists and accused them of promoting a kind of antiSemitism. He opposed the Balfour Paper and attempted to modify it. He clearly evidenced views that zionism and the creation of a Jewish state in Palestine would result in a racist state placing Jewish rights far above the rest of the people of Palestine who were not Jews. How clearly this situation described by Lord Montagu is demonstrated in Israel today.

Studying the history of zionism it is clear to see that zionism is the very antithesis of the heart and soul of the Jewish people and threatens to destroy them literally, as they are safer anywhere else in the world than Israel. Zionism is a very possible threat to the whole human race and the human race a hostage to it, as Israel refuses to make any concession to creating a real democracy in the region. In this situation, the threat of war continually looms, and in particular and as already stated, powers outside the region could become directly involved.

Israel is surely a prime example of how racism, practiced to any degree, in any way, shape or form, for any reason, by any one group against any other given group, will inevitably have the most destructive and devastating effect on that society.

Again and again, on close examination, from its inception to the current moment, the state of Israel has proven to have the most grave (and largely unaddressed) aspects, aspects that are undeniably immoral, deceitful, thoroughly unjust, and racist.

CHAPTER 44

If ever the world, and the whole international community were confronted with a brutal tyranny, it is surely the state of Israel. The "family of nations" desperately needs to place itself, united, and with the full weight of world responsibility behind it, in a common, worldwide opposition act decisively against Israel, a proven foe to human rights. Supporters of democracy can and must act against the state of Israel. Israel governance must be replaced with a real and solid democracy.

Further information that would amaze beyond belief most people in the west on the subject of Israel and the Palestinians is as follows from "Dissident Voice", August 2014:

"... Zionism has never had any qualms about the loss of Jewish lives so long as that loss furthered the cause of Zionism. In the book 51 Documents: Zionist Collaboration with the Nazis, editor Lenni Brenner, uses actual historic documents to demonstrate the betrayal of Jews by Zionists — before during, and after the Holocaust — even to the extent of offering to fight for the Nazis on the understanding that after Germany won the war, Zionism would be rewarded with Palestine." End of quote.

This book brings to light, through the use of actual historical documents, the (grave) disservice that zionists did to Jews before and during the holocaust. (Online description of the book).

Among these studies of zionist collaboration with Hitler, one encounters the word "holohoax." It is almost as if zionist collaboration with Hitler becomes subtly linked with holocaust denial. But the two issues are very far from each other. The former is based on exhaustive study, the later cannot produce definitive results.

It is possible to actually view internet videos in which alleged holocaust survivors speak about pianos and music performances during their stay in Auschwitz. One such survivor claims he was able with "vouchers" to buy whatever he needed at the cantina in Auschwitz. The people look to be exactly the age holocaust survivors would be. The interviews are conducted in all seriousness and although the people seem perfectly genuine, what they are saying in so outrageous one cannot help but wonder why, for what conceivable reason, these interviewees are lying. What is the reason such people would participate in these fake videos?

As I continued research into the truly bizarre world of holocaust denial, I looked at the figures of Jewish population worldwide, compiled by the International Red Cross during the years of the Second World War and published at the war's end. The report did not show a gap of 6,000,000 less but rather between 300,000 and 400,000 less Jewish people worldwide at the end of the war in 1944. When queried as to why the IRC figures did not show the loss of 6,000,000, in their report, the IRC said they were not responsible to the international community as census takers but as international health care workers. But the question then arises why would the IRC take upon itself to compile and publish figures that they then would, according to the Nuremberg Trials, be forced to disclaim?

CHAPTER 45

Other statistics from other agencies do show the missing six million Jewish lives lost during WWII. The Nizkor Project, which is a Canadian Jewish organization, compiled figures of upwards of five million Jews killed by the Nazis.

In 1942, a wealthy and prominent German industrialist met with Himmler and Eichmann, as well as other high-ranking nazi officers who informed the German of the plan by the Third Reich to destroy the Jews, Gypsies and other groups. In horror and shock the man, whose name was never disclosed, revealed to Gerald Reigner of the World Jewish Congress in Geneva, Switzerland this information. Gerald Reigner immediately contacted the American and British embassies who refused to believe him. Reigner then contacted the Red Cross, several board members of which he had developed close contact with. The members of the Red Cross were deeply shocked at the information of Regnier. In October 1942 at the Metropole Hotel in Geneva, while the extermination camps of Germany, Poland, Czechoslovakia, and the Ukraine were already coming into operation, the Board of the Red Cross met with the sole agenda of communicating directly to the world the devastating news of Hitler's extermination plans. The entire committee supported the plan to make public the findings. Madame Frick-Cramer made the statement, "The Committee simply cannot keep silent in the face of the worsening methods of war and extension of hostilities to the civilian population. If we keep quiet, we could risk the very existence of the Committee after the War."

All the Committee members agreed except one. Carl Burckhardt angrily claimed what the IRC proposed to do was "not courageous." That it would only enrage a "belligerent nation", by which he meant Germany. Philippe Etter spoke, then acting President of Switzerland who said that although he admired the initiative to inform the world of Hitler's plans, he feared that the Red Cross would lose its purported impartiality in its role as a caretaker to the nations and was not a political advisor in any case. Etter also stated his deep fear that Germany would easily decide to invade Switzerland in the event of such a damning omission on the part of the Red Cross. When the vote came all members of the Red Cross that day and in that meeting unanimously decided against revealing to the world public Hitler's true intentions to utterly eliminate the Jews as well as many other groups.

Carl Burckhardt, a Swiss-German, who later became the President of the Red Cross, had a great fear of communism and actually viewed nazi Germany as a wall against the Soviet Union.

In 1935, Burchhardt visited German concentration camps as a representative of the Red Cross and in his own words found them "hard but correct". One of the camps he visited was Dachau. In 1936 Burchhardt met with the nazi leadership. Afterward he wrote the warmest letter to Hitler saying how wonderful it had been to meet with him.

Records show that the figure of six million WWII Jewish deaths is attributed to Rudolf Hoess, (not to be confused with Rudolf Hess, a deputy of Hitler who went to Scotland in an attempt to end the war and was promptly arrested) the commander of Auschwitz who testified at the Nuremberg Trials that he overheard the figure given in conversation between Hitler and Goebbels. Goebbels informed Hitler, in this alleged conversation, Hoess claimed he overheard, that four million Jews had died in the concentration camps while two million had died in transit in trains (like cattle) between camps in the freezing cold of northern Europe and Russia. The entire testimony of Rudolf Hoess can be read on the internet.

However, other information collected from the files of Nuremberg Trial state that: "The (figure of six million) number seems to have first been mentioned by Dr. Wilhelm Hoettl, an Austrian-born official in the Third Reich and a trained historian who served in a number of senior positions in the SS.

In November 1945, Hoettl testified for the prosecution in the Nuremberg trials of accused Nazi war criminals. Later, in the 1961 trial in Israel of Adolf Eichmann, he also submitted to a lengthy series of questions from the prosecution, speaking under oath from a courtroom in Austria.

On both occasions, he described a conversation he had had with Eichmann, the SS official who had principal responsibility for the logistics of the Jewish genocide, in Budapest in August 1944. In the 1961 testimony, Hoettle, made statements to the effect that four million Jews had been gassed or otherwise died from starvation, disease, etc. in the camps themselves. Two million Jews had died, Eichmann claimed to Hoettl, en route in trains transporting them to the camps during winter in which circumstance many Jews also perished, Haaretz, May 2016.

Hitler had made numerous statements to the effect "of the necessity to exterminate the Jews" in well publicized speeches. Hoess states also that in 1941 he was summoned to Berlin to speak with Himmler who informed them that he and other commanders of the camps were to begin the process of "extermination of the Jews" and that this "project" was not to be revealed to anyone else whatsoever. When Hoess gave his information at the Nuremberg Trials, it is alleged by holocaust deniers that he did so because he was tortured or beaten up by allied Jewish officers, one of them being British Gerald Draper. The truth is Draper (who may or may not have been Jewish) interviewed Hoess extensively prior to being placed on trial in Nuremberg for the war crimes Hoess confessed to. But Draper used as calculating and as dispassionate a method as possible in extracting information from Hoess, the commander of Auschwitz. Never at at any time in these interrogations was Hoess subjected to anything but continuous and exhaustive questioning by Draper, completely unaccompanied by anything remotely connected to torture as Hoess cooperated fully with the allies, and gave full information of the atrocities committed at Auschwitz. Hoess did claim he had been beaten by the soldiers who discovered him in a barn disguised as a farmer when he resisted arrest and pretended he was not "Rudolf Hoess". One soldier demanded to see a ring Hoess was wearing. When Hoess said he could get it off, that it was stuck on his finger, the officer then threatened to cut off his finger. When finally Hoess removed it, the officer read on the inside of the ring, the full name of Rudolf Hoess. The way and the manner in which allied forces were able to locate Hoess was by information obtained from his wife. These soldiers did make the threat to Hoess's wife that if she refused to reveal his location, the British soldiers would abduct Hoess' son and turn him over to the Russians, who the allies said would torture the boy. At that point Hoess wife did disclose his location, in the countryside nearby. All this took place in Germany.

Hoess also changed his testimony at times, saying that one million and a half had died at Auschwitz, not four million. In 1948 a sign was placed in front of Auschwitz that on that site, four million Jews had perished. In 1989, the sign was replaced with the figure of one and a half million that had perished. Upon investigation it is unclear exactly who replaced the sign with the much lower figure. Was it the German government? Or another agency? The plaques apparently have been replaced by researchers who are affiliated with the Museum of Auschwitz-Birkenau.

Franciszek Piper, the former director of Auschwitz Museum, in 1980 wrote the following in an article on the official Auschwitz web site:

> "After an overall analysis of the original sources and findings on deportation to Auschwitz, I CONCLUDED that a total of at least 1,300,000 people were deported there, and that 1,100,000 of them perished. Approximately 200,000 people were deported from Auschwitz to other camps as part of the redistribution of labor resources and the final liquidation of the camp."

According to the Auschwitz Museum, no records of the number of prisoners who died at Auschwitz-Birkenau have ever been found. In an article on the official Auschwitz website, the former director, Franciszek Piper, wrote the following:

> "When the Soviet army entered the camp on January 27, 1945, they did not find any German documents (much had been destroyed already by the Nazis) there giving the number of victims, or any that could be used as a basis for calculating this number. Such documents (transport lists, notifications of the arrival of transports, reports about the outcome of selection) had been destroyed before liberation. For this reason, the Soviet commission investigating the crimes committed in Auschwitz Concentration Camp had to make estimates."

It appears after much exhaustive investigation over a period of several decades the figure of Jewish deaths are in dispute. Some research Jewish institutes of the holocaust, can still show up to seven million Jewish persons who perished in the holocaust, although most now claim a decreased figure of five million which is claimed can be proved by their research. But the full proofs and full figures to this day remain incomplete and in dispute, on both sides of the spectrum; those who claim a figure of around the original six million and holocaust deniers. According to numerous articles in Haaretz, a newspaper of respected journalistic standards and published daily in Israel, both groups are highly prejudiced in favor or their findings. Thus the real truth surrounding the actual figure of Jews who died in the holocaust still remains a mystery.

Four days before his death by hanging, Rudolf Hoess, wrote out this statement which was handed over to the state prosecutor; "My conscience compels me to make the following declaration. In the solitude of my prison cell I have come to the bitter recognition that I have sinned gravely against humanity. As Commandant of Auschwitz I was responsible for carrying out part of the cruel plans of the 'Third Reich' for human destruction. In so doing I have inflicted terrible wounds on humanity. I caused unspeakable suffering for the Polish people in particular. I am to pay for this with my life. May the Lord God forgive one day what I have done?"

Over a period of time from 1941 to 1944, trains carrying Jews, had arrived in Auschwitz, every four to six weeks, daily, holding cargoes all told, of two thousand people, from all over Europe and Hoess testified that with the exception of those considered strong enough to work, the rest of the Jews were gassed to death. Much of the gas chambers and the proof of mass extermination was destroyed by the Nazis themselves, as has been stated, including many of the cremation ovens, when the nazi high command realized they were losing the war. When Russian troops arrived they also demolished more of what remained in the camps.

Still, when General Patton liberated Auschwitz he was so horrified by what he saw that he demanded the whole town, some fifteen kilometers away from the actual camp, to march through it. At first the townspeople were suspicious and thought they were being forced to see something the allied soldiers "made up", but when the people from the nearby town saw the horrors of the camp, there was no doubt in their minds of the authenticity of Nazi "nightmare" stories. The mayor of the village and his wife went home and committed suicide. Holocaust deniers claim that there were no facilities sufficiently large, or evident at the time of allied troops on their first entry to the camps, to destroy the bodies of so many people alleged to being killed on a daily basis. There were a reported only fifteen ovens in the crematorium when Auschwitz was liberated. Again, most historians and researchers say that many ovens were removed before allied forces arrived to liberate the camps, and it was publicly known that much of the implements of death had been destroyed or removed. But there were huge "death pits" covered with bars through which one could see decomposing bodies. It was not possible to see how many victims were actually placed there or how deep these pits were. People today say that even the birds don't sing there in Auschwitz. It seems that even creatures of nature avoid creating their nests in Auschwitz or are able to live there at all.

The final answer to holocaust deniers is that if any or all of their allegations as to the falsification of the holocaust were true, then the over 166 German nazi officers, including Rudolf Hoess, who led and oversaw all the atrocities at Auschwitz would have denied the accusations to the hilt. Yet none of them ever did. Instead they supplied the Nuremberg Court with countless names and dates of the Nazi atrocities that took place between 1939 and 1944. And the fact is, all these men had absolutely nothing to lose in denying the allegations since they all, to a man, faced life imprisonment or the death penalty. None of these German men, former nazi officers, ever once even hinted that any of the allegations were false.

Further quotes from Dissident Voice, issue of August, 2014 include:

"If I knew that it was possible to save all the children of Germany by transporting them to England, and only half by transporting them to the Land of Israel, I would choose the latter, for before us lies not the numbers of these children, but the historic reckoning of the people of Israel."

— From Israeli historian Shabtai Teveth's book on Ben-Gurion.

Further quotes from Dissident Voice, August 2014:

"Zionist Apartheid Israel's deliberate long-term policy of periodic military attacks against the largely unarmed Palestinian people — including the current cowardly and barbarous attacks has absolutely nothing to do with "self-defense" because even the pitiful Hamas rocket attacks are rendered ineffective by Israel's American taxpayer-funded Iron Dome Missile Shield. The real reason for such attacks is to fulfill Zionist ideology by avoiding any kind of negotiated peace that might forestall the illegal Israeli land grabs and ethnic cleansing required for the creation of a "Greater Israel" devoid of Palestinians."

Although it does need to be stated that Israel, to a very large degree if not completely, has given up the idea of a "Greater Israel" once espoused by Ariel Sharon and others, even Ben Gurion himself. There may exist some in power who would espouse a greater Israel but have given up the idea for the sake of political expediency. Still, such persons who would even inwardly countenance such ideas should not remain in power in Israel, as such predilections highly dangerous.

Again from Dissident Voice:

"To add insult to injury, these unashamed Zionist savages also have the barefaced audacity to refer to Palestinians as "animals" and to themselves as "God's Chosen People." History has repeatedly shown that whenever one ethnic group regards itself as being superior to others — be it a "Master Race" or a "Chosen People" — then after much death and destruction it will eventually perish as was the case with the Third Reich."

'Zionist Israel's evil racist intentions have remained constant ever since its inception with its primary founder and first Prime Minister, David BenGurion emphatically stating that "We must use terror, assassination, intimidation, land confiscation, and the cutting of all social services to rid the Galilee of its Arab population." This "Father of the nation" and now (if there is an afterlife) guest of the Devil, must be very proud of the tenacity with which his "God-Chosen" compatriots have stuck to their task by pillaging and murdering their way southwards into the West Bank and Gaza Strip.

The successful selling to the world of blatant Israeli lies and fabricated justifications has been achieved by an assault on all possible fronts including the gross distortion of archaeological facts and Biblical narrative.'

> *"Appropriations of the past as part of the politics of the present . . . could be illustrated for most parts of the globe. One further example which is of particular interest to this study, is the way in which archeology and biblical history have become of such importance to the modern state of Israel. It is this combination which has been such a powerful factor in silencing Palestinian history."*

— Keith W. Whitela, Dissident Voice, August 2014

CHAPTER 46

It is critical to note that much of "Biblical" justification for the state of Israel has been contrived and distorted. The books on the subject by Dr. Naim Ateek, the Anglican priest and director of Sabeel Seminary reveal in detail these distortions. An outstanding work by Dr. Ateek on this subject is, "A Palestinian Theology of Liberation: The Bible Justice and the PalestinianIsraeli Conflict.

Not to mention, the verse in Psalms which says "The earth is the Lord's and the fullness thereof". It is therefore obvious, if you want to go by the Bible that the whole planet belongs to God and not any one of us.

To continue with further quotations from the same publication, "Dissident Voice",

> "De-Arabizing the history of Palestine is another crucial element of the ethnic cleansing. 1500 years of Arab and Muslim rule and culture in Palestine are trivialized, evidence of its existence is being destroyed and all this is done to make the absurd connection between the ancient Hebrew civilization and today's Israel. The most glaring example of this today is in Silwan, (Wadi Hilweh) a town adjacent to the Old City of Jerusalem with some 50,000 residents. Israel is expelling families from Silwan and destroying their homes because it claims that King David built a city there some 3,000 years ago. Thousands of families will be made homeless so that Israel can build a park to commemorate a king that may or may not have lived 3,000 years ago. Not a shred of historical evidence exists that can prove King David ever lived yet Palestinian men, women, children and the elderly along with their schools and mosques, churches and ancient cemeteries and any evidence of their existence must be destroyed and then denied so that Zionist claims to exclusive rights to the land may be substantiated."

— Miko Peled, Israeli peace activist and author (Born Jerusalem, 1961)

"The most successful Zionist ploy has been to equate itself with Judaism and to hijack and hide behind Judaic aspects starting with sacred emblems such as the Menorah and then to demean the memory of the Holocaust whose constant, cynical invocation is used to silence criticism of barbaric Israeli crimes and even to evoke illusory justification for the cold, calculated genocide of the Palestinian people.

> *'Israelis and American Jews fully agree that the memory of the Holocaust is an indispensable weapon — one that must be used relentlessly against their common enemy ... Jewish organizations and individuals thus labor continuously to remind the world of it. In America, the perpetuation of the Holocaust memory is now a $100-million-a-year enterprise, part of which is government funded.'*

"The continued use of "anti-Semitism" as a weapon against its critics — even to the extent of the recent invention of a "New anti-Semitism" — is essential for the survival of Zionism because it serves to deflect attention from the lying, cheating, stealing, murdering, war profiteering, blatant violations of international law, and barbaric crimes against humanity. Yet despite such overwhelming and irrefutable evidence of Israel's unabated criminality, Jews everywhere continue to decline from equating Zionism with Judaism, and most of those who do recognize the difference, lack the courage to say so; the corporate mass media continues to refuse to do the right thing by unconditionally reporting the facts; so-called political leaders — led by Israel's "Uncle Tom" Barack Obama and Canada's noxiously obsequious Prime Minister, Stephen Harper — continue with blinkered eyes to fawn over and commend Israel's ethnic cleansing of the Palestinian people; and as for the most of the rest of us, by quietly accepting Israel's propaganda lies, we become complicit in its crimes while obediently supping from a Zionist trough that is overflowing with Palestinian blood."

The above information is excerpted from an online publication, "Dissident Voice" in an article by Charles A. Weisman, issued August 14, 2014.

Speaking with a friend who visited Israel, many years ago, he made the remark, "that situation will never work"!

Truly, how can any observer by any remote stretch of the imagination countenance Israel as a political resolution that is benefiting the Jewish people?

It is ludicrous to read about some Jewish people who seem to think they will die if they don't control Palestine, such as Ariel Sharon, "Jews have nowhere to go". The actual fact is that the greatest portion of world Jewish population is concentrated in the United States where Jews live far more safely than in Israel. Jews who immigrate to Israel have to live in a deathfilled environment where their lives are constantly endangered because of the obsessive desire on the part of these Jews to dominate the Holy Land.

Ben Gurion is often quoted as saying, "the old ones will die and the young will forget", in a reference to Palestinian reaction to the state of Israel. The observer cannot help but wonder what kind of crazy, mixed-up person would imagine that the Arabs of Palestine were so "retarded", so simple-minded, they would eventually passively, simply acquiesce a great portion of their homeland (if not all of it) to another people, which homeland the people and their ancestors had lived in for two thousand years.

The fact is, Ben Gurion's statement reflects a view of the Palestinians that cannot be interpreted as anything other than racist.

Ben Gurion never imagined or countenanced what would occur instead, (of a supposed Palestinian acquiescence to the Jewish state) a long protracted "war" in the region with seemingly no end. Not to mention the amount of Israeli dissidents inside Israel, who, through their organizations, constantly disclaim the injustice and tyranny of their own government.

The United States government hands over to the government of Israel between three and nine billion dollars yearly. The U.S. government demands that Israel buy from them, with part of that money, armaments, weaponry of various sorts, and helicopters to be used by the IDF, according to articles in Time and other news magazines.

CHAPTER 47

It is beyond belief that American taxpayers should foot the bill for Israel s continuing injustice and the cruelty perpetrated every day against Palestinians. Bulldozing houses, destroying property, beating resistant homeowners and detaining Palestinians at checkpoints and brutalizing them, according to B TSelem, on a monthly basis, simply for trying to reach their places of employment inside Israel, and causing them to live in a constant, abject state of fear. This is what American taxpayers are paying for.

Instead, and at the very opposite end of the political spectrum, the United States and its citizens should be working in every conceivable way to open the door and create a pathway for democracy in Israel and the West Bank, and now Gaza. Although this sentiment has been stated previously, it cannot be said and advocated enough.

The statement, widespread, on the part of Israeli Jews that all of the world Jewry supports Israel, is in fact, grossly distorted. From the early part of the last century to the present, many and numerous Jews and groups of Jews have expressed extreme discomfort at the idea of zionism and an exclusive Jewish state. The reasons were and have been solidly stated in the writings of Lord Montagu, the second British Jew to be elected to Parliament in England, and third Jew to be elected to the British Cabinet. Montagu opposed zionism and called it anti-semitic. His views continue to the present day among members of the organization in England, "Jews for Palestinian Justice".

Zionism, is, in fact, nothing more than a hysterical cult based on purely destructive emotionalism and not on facts, as Israel attempts to blot out the whole region of Palestine and its history. Palestinian history is proven to be as long if not longer in the region, and stretches back to the most ancient Canaanite tribes, as do the Jews. Both groups are Semitic.

In NSWAS, the residents showed us the gas masks stored in case of another massive attack by Arab countries while we were seated in the dining room. There were even small gas masks for children. On visitor nearly wept when he saw them. I tried to explain that the Jews don't have to live in that region, they are choosing this situation. What kind of people would put their own children and babies in this crisis situation solely for the cause of Jewish nationalism? The Jews I met in NSWAS were highly educated people as are most Israelis. They could all easily be living anywhere in the west, in the U.S., Europe and other countries, safely, as has been noted many times.

After the six day war, the media reported an account of an American official walking with Ben Gurion near the now occupied West Bank. When the American pleaded with Ben Gurion to leave the West Bank and discontinue the military occupation of the West Bank by Israel, Ben Gurion refused. "Not even for peace", the exasperated official asked in dismay.

"No", Ben Gurion replied "not even for peace".

The fact is it has been noted by many journalists that the reality is there is no government in Israel, on either the Likud or Labor side, that seriously supports a fully autonomous Palestinian state.

Many international observers of the region find it bewildering that the zionists return to Palestine was concomitant with a return to its most primitive and barbaric past. In order to maintain the Jewish state it was necessary to become involved in the most bloody and terrible wars. How on earth did this benefit the Jewish people, and more importantly, how does this situation ensure their safety, which was the whole reason for a Jewish state to begin with?

In the early 1900's the first Jewish settlers went to live in Palestine and form their collective communities, the kibbutzs. Many were socialists (obviously not the ones in the WSO Golda Meir spoke to mentioned previously) and intellectuals, who really believed in the possibility of peacefully living with the Arabs and creating, at the same time, a Jewish state.

All too quickly the dreams of the zionists turned into nightmares for Palestinians as zionist terror began the cold-blooded murders committed by the Irgun and the Stern Gang. After the massacres at Deir Yassin, Ben Gurion disavowed all knowledge of the horrors that occurred that day in the small village. Immediately after the massacres he had received a letter from the then King Abdullah of Jordan asking how such atrocities occurred. Ben Gurion simply said he didn't know anything about what happened. All too easy for Ben Gurion to do. Why could he not control the horrors practiced by these terrorist gangs? Or did he keep silent on their actions because the terror campaign was working, many Arabs were fleeing Palestine. With the west squarely behind him, Israel was after all, comprised of and empowered by western people. In this sense, Ben Gurion already held reins of real power in the Middle East.

Just as the world was so endangered by the nazi threat as it moved inexorably through europe, so the world is threatened by the state of Israel. If another war breaks out in that region, such a war would inevitably, this time, suck the whole world into a nuclear nightmare.

A case can be made that the state of Israel itself is the worst form of anti-Semitism. In order to have a Jewish state the rights of Palestinians were destroyed, or greatly diminished, to say the least. All the history of humanism and ethics produced uniquely by Jews in the west simply and suddenly ceased to exist. And a "zionist entity" as the Arabs refer to the state of Israel took the place of the late great Jewish people.

CHAPTER 48

I read of a Palestinian poet living in the United States in Modesto, California, an area not far from where I myself grew up in northern California. In a TV interview he quietly advocated a Palestinian state. The man was a recognized poet both in Palestine and the U.S. and definitely non-violent in his beliefs. The man was widely thought to have been murdered by the JDL, Jewish "Defense" League, a terrorist organization. His name was Alex Odeh and he was an American Palestinian. His tragic death occurred in 1985. Though many civil rights groups attempted to bring to justice his murderers and the FBI named the JDL as responsible for his death, his killers have never been identified.

The fact is I never heard an Arab say that Jews from the west had no right to come to Palestine. What I did hear from Palestinians was that Jews from the west had no right to come to their country, arm themselves and then proceed to drive the people out of their homes and create a political system that virtually disenfranchised non-Jewish Palestinians from every aspect of the infrastructure the zionists proceeded to develop, making the Arabs of Palestine either stateless persons or second class citizens (if they were lucky enough to receive Israeli citizenship) in their own homeland. It is also curious, to call the war the zionists made against the Arabs, a "War of Independence". It is a strange idea to try to make yourself independent from the very people and place your military has overtaken and occupied.

I spent an afternoon in Acre, a beautiful town along the coast in the very far north of Israel, as is Safed. Acre has a very long history, stretching back to the Crusades when it was a very active port. I sat in a cafe where I could look out at the brightly painted boats of the local fisherman docked along the quay. As I sat having a snack, I glanced up at the group of Palestinian men who I thought might be the owners.

The three men stared at me stonily. One man had deep pain etched on his face as our eyes met. It was as though he was looking at me for an answer to a deeply disturbing question which he had searched for in vain. This was a moment that was one of the most unusual in my life. Right in front of my eyes I saw, the suffering and deep personal loss this man and the others sitting with him had experienced, which came about because of the Israeli occupation and wars made against Arabs. Because I was not dressed as an Arab, he could see I was from somewhere in the west, perhaps even Israel. I had to sit and look directly into the faces of those who had experienced Israeli domination, something the entire west had supported, and the brutal wars displacing so many of his people. Arabs and Jews lived together for centuries in Palestine, and to this day, no Palestinian understands why this partition between Arab and Jew ever came about. It is incomprehensible to Arabs. The moment of staring into the eyes of that man in Acre, made me responsible for the rest of my life. Ever since my travels in the Middle East I have been compelled to speak to whoever will listen that, in occupying Arab territories and forcing a separatist Jewish state on the region, Israel has committed a wrong that will not easily be righted, if it will be possible at all. It was in Acre that in 1948 more Arabs were expelled than in any other area of Palestine. At the time of my visit to Acre in 1995, I did walk into a large, densely packed area of older houses with many Arab people living there. It was clear that Arab Acre still existed in spite of the grievous depravations of the war in 1948.

Another real conflict in historic Palestine, as it is now referred to, is not between Arab and Jew. It is between east and west. There is a huge culture gap between all the people of the Holy Land, including the Jews who have been living there for a very long times, since the diaspora in 70 AD, and the Jews from the west. When the Jews or zionists came from the west with their political agenda to establish a Jewish state, they came, in reality, as westerners, first and foremost. Because these Jews brought with them the backing and the political power of the west, since the whole west eventually came to support the zionists. The zionists also brought the great expertise of the west. It can be said that ultimately the zionists became tools of the west, and a very real part of western expansionism, not to mention U.S. hegemony.

I looked up some friends of a friend in Mallorca while visiting the yearly flower festival in Haifa. The festival reminded me of the cherry blossom festival in Japan, which, although I have never visited Japan, heard much about, since it is a subject from my studies of Japanese painting.

The Kourey family, very much involved in Haifa life for generations greeted me warmly. I had called them from my hostel the night before and they had immediately asked me to lunch. Lunch was delicious and the only thing wrong with it was that it was over so quickly. I was taken by Mrs. Kourey, actually from Italy, on a tour of Daliat where we shopped together in the stalls of white-robed Muslim men. Mrs. Kourey told me again what I had heard before, that this particular group of Muslims were thought to have come from Turkey a long time ago. They also practiced a form of Islam that included the doctrine of reincarnation. Their past was clouded in mystery and no one was sure how many centuries these people had lived in northern Israel. An unusual component of the region, some sources cite the establishment of the Druze, "colony", (how the people are referred to) as taking place in the eleventh century by an Egyptian ruler, who was a devout Muslim.

I was told at lunch that Mr. Kourey's family came from Lebanon to Palestine 750 years ago. They were Roman Catholics. Mrs. Kourey had taken me to their church with the hopes that I could meet their pastor or "father". I did not meet him but she told me that he was a great scholar and very interesting and special to speak to about church history and about the region's past.

Mrs. Kourey accounted to me a story of Palestinian friends who lived on the border of Israel near the West Bank. Israeli authorities actually confiscated their house one day citing "security reasons". I asked if they were compensated for their sudden and irrevocable loss of property. "They did not receive a cent", Mrs. Kourey replied.

Though Christian and Arab (Mr. Kourey being Arab) Mrs. Kourey said they had many Israeli friends, mostly secular, who she and her family visited with frequently. She thought it was a mystery that the Israeli government refused to come to a serious political compromise with the Palestinians. "We know many Israelis who support a Palestinian state", she said.

It is an obvious fact of Israeli life that Israelis live in up to standard homes surrounded with greenery and have good infrastructure, i.e., school, hospitals available to them. Israelis are well shielded from the horrors and devastation in the West Bank and Gaza. The Occupied Territories might as well be far away as Mars for all the contact Israelis have with these areas or knowledge of its inhabitants.

I spoke with a number of Palestinians who said that they knew numerous Israelis who expressed a strong interest in doing business with them, the Palestinians, but the Israeli government's heavy restrictions limits Palestinians from doing so, and in so doing limits Israel's capacity for having commercial relations with Palestinian businesses only a few miles away.

Late in the afternoon I thanked Mrs. Kourey for the wonderful time she and her husband had shown me, as she dropped me off at the bus station to take the trip back up to NSWAS, outside Jerusalem. She told me that the family had a small place where I could stay if I needed it, should I visit Haifa again. And I warmly thanked her for her and her husband's wonderful hospitality.

CHAPTER 49

Today many people seek out "spiritual truths" that transcend or go beyond religious ideas. The idea "that everything has a reason for happening" has become prevalent among these seekers. I have certainly thought of spiritual lessons in terms of the unrelenting crisis in the Middle East.

So many times I have thought that the spiritual lesson for the Israelis is to treat the Palestinians as if they are Jews. Aside from the spiritual power in such action, it is probably true. All Semitic people can trace their genetic inheritance back to the most ancient Canaanite tribes, as spoken of earlier.

I read an article from Haaretz, the newspaper published daily in Tel Aviv, about a think tank in Israel headed by a man named Uri Dromo. In their studies this think tank concluded that all the people of the region, Jews from the west as well as all Palestinians were derived from the earliest Canaanite tribes and were all, genetically the same. Israelis did not take the reports seriously or were amused, and the Palestinians angrily denied the results.

I was buying an ice cream cone in Jerusalem while waiting for the bus to take me back to NSWAS. A conversation was struck up and the girl that handed me my ice cream cone said that her brother was out on "duty" at the moment. As we spoke about the wars in the region, the girl suddenly looked grim. I wasn't sure what, but I had said something that had caused her to completely close up. I remembered a report I read about the capture of 1,000 Arab men during one of the wars in the Sinai. The report had gone on to say, that although the men were captured, Israeli forces slaughtered all of them to a man even though they had been captured and were unarmed. I knew that our discussion of all Israeli men having to be "on call" and go out at least once a month on military duty had triggered a memory that the girl I spoke to, wanted to forget. In spite of the loveliness of the weather, the city and the people, I had a terrible feeling. Terrible things happened to Jews, including their incarceration in the death camps of Germany and then in camps in Cyprus. But many Jews were beginning to be horrified by what they were required to do militarily, to "keep the Israeli state alive".

In my mind's eye, I saw, so to speak, Yitzhak Rabin after this death. I saw many Arab people he had killed in wars, their ghostly images closing in on him. And he cannot, in these images, he simply cannot understand in this after- death state, why he killed these people or why he had ordered others to have them killed. The deaths of these Palestinians make absolutely no sense to him. Absolutely none. The spirit of Prime Minister Rabin is cast into a living hell of "not understanding". Spirits of those slain Arabs unrelentingly pass before his "eyes". And no matter how hard he struggles, he now realizes that there was no sense in their deaths, whatsoever.

Historic Palestine has been the focal point for critical and important events over centuries. It is as though if the earth were a body, Jerusalem and its surroundings are its pulse point, making everything occurring in its proximity to be intensified by its invisible, yet very real "pulse".

Another amazing example of the truly mysterious aspect of the Holy Land, is a story I read on the internet that recounted the most unusual experiences of peoples visting the region. The story described two men on leave from a U.S. Navy ship at anchor in the port of Haifa, Israel. They had bought tickets for a tour of Jerusalem and Bethlehem. There is much excavation in the depths of the Old City and they described, (as I myself have seen) four or five, sometimes up to six layers of the city which had been built over time literally, on top of each other. As they looked down at the reconstruction of an old Roman Street in the middle of the Old City, one man Rook, suddenly looked up at Tom, his fellow Navy officer, in shock. Tom surprised, listened as Rook came over and told him what he had seen. I saw you down there in a Roman robe and you stared right up at me as if you recognized me. Completely stunned, neither man knew what to say or think. As their tour continued they went into the basement of the Church of the Nativity in Bethlehem where Christians believe Jesus had laid in the manger as depicted in the New Testament. The tour guide explained that all stables were often constructed below buildings so that the horses and animals could be placed there out of sight and also create warmth that would rise up and provide heat for the human living space above. Suddenly, Tom saw, in a kind of vision, a baby girl. Immediately he knew his wife was pregnant. When he called her later that evening, she did in fact, confirm that she was pregnant. "Her name is Patricia Ruth", Tom told his wife. Their daughter was indeed born, but she was still born, dead on delivery. Tom and his wife subsequently had another baby girl who did live and became the portended Patricia Ruth. Both men were devout evangelical Christians. Neither believed in reincarnation and although the baby girl died that Tom "saw" in the church, Tom believed that God has a purpose in everything. Both Tom and Rook were deeply affected by these experiences and neither one had any explanation for them.

CHAPTER 50

One day in Ramallah, I stepped into a group taxi on the way to another visit of Beir Zeit University. I got into a conversation with a young guy, Tariq, who was a student there and on his way to classes. As we left Ramallah, we entered an area of land which appeared to be almost deserted. Our group taxi was the only car on the road for some miles as we passed barren, large brown hills, some of them very high. They were devoid of vegetation or any sign of animals that might be grazing on the hilltops. Tariq told me that he lived with his family in Jericho. He described where he lived and invited me to visit his family and have lunch with them the following day. I happily agreed.

Following Tariq's instructions, I arrived the next day, found the house across from a garage and big tire shop, just as he had described. When Tariq saw me, I could see him coming quickly out of the house to greet me. We went inside and he introduced me to his family. His dad sat quietly on the couch. He did not say anything at all during my visit. I had the impression he had some illness. I thought perhaps Tariq's father had not been able to get necessary treatment due to the occupation. I met his mom, a very nice lady, who, although looking a bit tired, warmly shook my hand. Then I met Nevin, a very pretty and interesting girl of about twenty or so. Everybody wanted to know all about my travels, and what I was doing, as I traveled around the West Bank. I told them how compelling the area was for me and how much I was enjoying visiting it. And I thanked them again for asking me, a total stranger, to have lunch with them. As we passed into the dining room to sit down and have lunch, I glanced down at a plaque of Palestine. That was it. Just a map of old Palestine, carved out of a piece of wood and painted, what most people referred to as the "Holy Land", for centuries. There was no sign or indication of Israel at all. This plaque with its depiction of Palestine and no sign of Israel on it was, yet again, another "telling" statement I encountered on my travels in the region. In the minds of almost all Palestinians, Israel simply does not exist.

What is there, or what the rest of the world views as Israel, will, in the minds of Palestinians, in time, "just go away".

Lunch was hot and very tasty. We were served bowls filled with vegetables, salad, and roast beef. When we returned to the living room we watched "Al Jazeera" TV. The program reviewed the massacres at Deir Yassin. When Tariq turned to me and remarked about these horrors, I could hardly look at him. The whole experience of confronting the reality of the atrocities committed that day and the fact that no one knows who perpetrated these atrocities or was ever brought to justice, made me go sickeningly blank. It was no different than seeing a mob in the American south lynching a black man in a room filled with black people. I shrank from the horror of the fact that there was no way to recompense a people wronged to such an extent. In both cases the wrong is too great. We can only hope and pray that enough hearts change and enough legal bodies in the world make war criminals and those guilty of atrocities pay and pay dearly. Tariq stared at me quizzically when all I could do was acknowledge I had heard of these horrible atrocities. It was a truly chilling experience.

I then asked Nevin why she didn't wear a headscarf, or hijab. She replied, "oh no, not for me." Neither did Tariq's mother wear a hijab. In the middle of our conversation, another sister of Tariq came in the room. She was fully dressed in the now traditional clothing Muslim women wear. She was covered from head to toe in heavy cloth and wearing a hijab on her head and around her throat. She stared at me as if I had dropped down from outer space. As we spoke, Tariq's sister explained, a little timidly I thought, that she worked in one of Jericho's complex of businesses, in "customer service" she said. That was the only English she spoke. The rest of our conversation was translated by Tariq and Nevin. It came time for Tariq to take me to the local ruins in Jericho which he had promised to do. I asked Nevin if she would accompany us. "No", said Tariq. "It is not good for her to go out". I tried to find out why he thought this, but there seemed to be no further discussion on the matter and reluctantly she turned from us and went back into the house. I was not very happy with this situation, but had no choice since I was a guest, to follow the brisk gait of Tariq toward the ruins. It was very hot. Above the excavations was a cafe up above the ruins. It was a climb to get up to the cafe but sitting in it, it was possible to see the Dead Sea. Everything is so close in the area, the "Holy Land". You have only to go a few miles in any direction to enter a wholly different region and completely different cultures and people, as well as enter the most ancient and famous historical sites.

After a few hours in the blazing heat, I thanked Tariq who waited for me to get the group taxi back to Ramallah and then on to Jerusalem. We had seen many shops with Arab artifacts and a lot of graffiti on walls depicting Yassir Arafat. As we sat waiting in the intense afternoon heat, I thought of what Tariq had said about the hijab and conservative dress, "good for winter" but not, he honestly concluded, the rest of the time.

I met Tariq on another occasion in Beir Zeit, along with other students and friends of his. I will never forget when I arrived in the packed student union, how I could hear overhead, an echo that almost sounded like Arab music or an Arab chant. It was the most amazing sound and experience. It was simply the rise of voices of all those students present, to the ceiling, which then held our voices and somehow made them into a kind of music.

IN CLOSING

Upon my return to Mallorca where I lived in the 1990's, from my visit to Palestine, I tried many times to contact Tariq, Nevin and the rest of the family. It was then 2001 and the Second Intifada had begun. I sent letters to them with pictures of us visiting together that day after lunch in their garden, which were complete with the goat they had tied at the rear of the garden. But I did not hear from them, due to problems in infrastructure in the West Bank caused by the Intifada. I only got recordings when i tried to call. I was very sad to lose contact.

The Middle East conflict is truly a devil's knot. The harder you try to loosen it, the tighter it becomes.

There are prominent orthodox Jews referred to earlier, the Neturei Karta, that disavow the current Israel of today. They believe that only the Messiah can restore the state of Israel. Some groups of Evangelical Christians now believe the same. Only the Second Coming can bring about the restoration of the state of Israel, they believe. The "true state of Israel", in the minds of some visionaries, reaches far beyond ethnicity, politics or human logic. When that True State is born, not one drop of blood will be shed.

The impact around the world of Israel and Palestine completely united, spiritually and politically would be unimaginably profound. Truly, such a transformation in the Middle East would transform the whole world.

ABOUT THE AUTHOR

I grew up in northern California in what has once the heart of the Gold Rush. I have lived in New York City where I studied art and also published poetry in various journals I have lived in Mallorca, Spain, France, Turkey and Mexico. I am currently residing in Vallejo, California, the place of my birth.

Printed in the United States
By Bookmasters